Julia Latchem-Smith was born in Basildon, Essex, in 1981. She now lives in Bridgend, South Wales, with her husband Jonathan and their three children Molly, Katelyn and Zack.

Daddy's little girl

JULIA LATCHEM-SMITH

headline
review

First published in 2007 by HEADLINE REVIEW
An imprint of Headline Publishing Group

First published in paperback in 2007 by HEADLINE REVIEW

4

Cataloguing in Publication Data is available from the British Library

978 0 7553 1638 0

Typeset in Dante by Avon DataSet Ltd,
Bidford-on-Avon, Warwickshire

Printed and bound in Great Britain by
Mackays of Chatham plc, Chatham, Kent

Headline's policy is to use papers that are natural, renewable and recyclable
products and made from wood grown in sustainable forests. The logging and
manufacturing processes are expected to conform to the environmental
regulations of the country of origin.

HEADLINE PUBLISHING GROUP
An Hachette Livre UK Company
338 Euston Road
London NW1 3BH

www.reviewbooks.co.uk
www.hodderheadline.com

For my husband, Jonathan, whose love,
support and determination has given me
the strength to find my own.

This is a true story but some names and
identifying characteristics have been changed
to protect the subjects' identities.

Contents

Acknowledgements

So many people played a part in the journey I have taken to seek justice, and resolution to my past. A few I want to thank personally for the support they have given. First and foremost my husband and his family, for never doubting me. Not once have any of you turned your backs on me, even when times were hard. I thank each and every one of you for your support and love. I regard you all as my own family rather than as in-laws. To Yvonne Bailey, for helping me to understand that life is about the journey and not so much the destination, for your support throughout the trial, and your love as a friend. And finally to Robert Inkster, whose dedication to the case was outstanding. From start to finish you were there for Jonathan and me, giving us hope when we felt we had none left. We shall always regard you as a dear friend. To everyone else I haven't mentioned but who played a part in this journey, you know who you are, and that you will always be in my heart.

Introduction

Children are taught from a very young age the difference between right and wrong, good and bad. Every word and every action a parent teaches a child influences the person that child will become. When those parental messages are faulty, imagine how a growing child can be affected.

My childhood made me a very fragmented person. The sexual and emotional abuse to which I was subjected for years conditioned me to such an extent that I had no comprehension of right or wrong, good or bad. I understood only the reality in which I lived, where morals and values were distorted, leaving me unsure of my place in the world.

Often, when I was a child, people such as teachers and friends' parents commented that I was 'odd', that my behaviour was 'strange'. The double existence I was forced to live left me struggling to adjust to life outside the home. Battling against my distorted view of reality, I became destructive not only to myself, but also to those around me. Years of denial left me accepting my past as normal, so that I was unable to face the truth about my parents' actions. But the blunt reality finally became something from which I could no longer hide so that I embarked on a journey where I was forced to determine my own morals, every day having to stand up for what is 'right', even though it was easier to live with what was 'wrong'. In a struggle to find justice in a world still coming to terms with the reality of child abuse, I fought against those who would prefer to turn a blind eye. So many people still choose to live in oblivion rather than accept the facts of abuse. I became determined to expose the truth, and the costs of living as a victim. Only now, years later, can I rationalise the true effect that growing up in a dysfunctional family had on me, and begin to learn how to progress with my life. I am still slowly undoing the knots of deceit that my childhood tied.

I have had to recondition my thoughts, beliefs and values in order to become a whole human being and to be able to function in a world where my parents' values are, as I have finally discovered, far from normal.

People ask me how I have healed myself. I can only respond that I now know how to function for myself. My eyes have been opened to a world which, until recently, I hardly knew existed. As an adult I have had to decide which path to take, and take the necessary steps to remove negativity from my life, however close I may have been to the people presenting it. On a journey of self-discovery and awareness, I have realised that the truth really does set you free.

This is my story . . .

I

The Calm before the Storm

Suzanne sat quietly in her chair as I poured her tea. A wave of pride washed over me as I chatted away to my audience. Every word I spoke was unquestioned; every gaze uninterrupted.

I smoothed down a crease in Suzanne's dress with such love it physically hurt inside my chest. I couldn't imagine a more perfect moment. I pondered this, and decided that, actually, some cake or chocolate biscuits would be a rather nice way to round off this tea party. I decided I would definitely aim to have some next time.

A splashing noise broke through my thoughts and alerted me to the fact that I had overfilled the teacup. Water was covering the table.

'Julia! Let me clear that up now! Time to put that tea set and dolls away.' My mother's voice penetrated through from the kitchen. The moment was lost.

I was seven years old and grateful to have been allowed to play with real water in my tea set. It wasn't usual to have such freedom in the house, and I was determined to do as I was told for fear that the privilege wouldn't be repeated. I helped to pack away without complaint. Mum liked her house to be kept neat and tidy at all times. Many things in my own room I had never touched in my life. At night I would lie staring at the teddies, in their original little bags, sitting on my bedroom shelves. I often wondered if I dare climb up to touch them, but the fear of what might happen to me if I was caught kept me in my bed. Mum hated anything to be touched in case I made a mess. If I was found to be 'fiddling' with things, the row that would follow was not worth the risk. It was almost as though some toys were kept for decoration. Others were 'allowed', for some reason, with minimal toys allocated for 'playing purposes'. These I loved with a passion. This was how it was with Suzanne.

Suzanne was my favourite doll. It didn't matter that her arm had been sewn on time and again. She was mine and I loved her unconditionally; as I thought any mother should love her child.

Every penny I had, Christmas and birthdays, was spent on her. I remember queuing in Mothercare after carefully deciding on an item of clothing to suit her, oblivious to the curious looks of the shop assistants. The dolls' clothes in the toy section were inadequate for

Suzanne; only the newborn range of 'proper' clothes would do.

For as long as I could remember having Suzanne, I dreamed of the day that I myself would become a mother and imagined the delight I would feel at having a child of my own – someone to spoil, to love, to cherish.

Dreamily I would answer the question I was always asked by my aunties and uncles.

'What would you like to be when you grow up, Julia?'

'I just want to be a mum . . .'

They would laugh at my naïvety, relishing my youthful ignorance. I had no idea what motherhood really meant.

I would often take Suzanne to my nanna's for the day. I spent a lot of time with my mother's mother. Nanna would catch a glimpse of Suzanne from the corner of her eye and, for a split second, gasp in horror in the mistaken belief that a real baby was lying on the floor. This both excited and annoyed me. I revelled in the idea that my nanna thought her so lifelike, but at the same time I was angry that anyone could possibly question the authenticity of my poor baby.

At that time, we lived in Church End Lane in Runwell, a small village in Essex and Nanna lived just a couple of miles away. I spent a lot of time with her. I always felt very close to her and she always welcomed me with open arms. I loved the smell of mint sauce from her kitchen as she cooked a Sunday dinner. I was more at home in her home than in my own.

My parents had married in 1970 when my mum was just eighteen. They had my older brother, Paul, in 1979, and sixteen months later, I followed.

Mum was thirty-six years old when I was seven and my story begins. She was a nervous woman who was very easily stressed. She had barely ever worked since meeting my dad at college. Straight after marriage she had become a housewife.

Mum was always rather cold with Paul and me. She wasn't the type of parent who would get down on the floor and play games, or run around chasing us and laughing, as my dad did. But, as a small child, I just accepted what she was like, and revelled instead in the endless enthusiasm that my dad showed for me.

Dad was forty when I was seven. For as long as I can remember he worked in the financial services industry, offering advice on such schemes as investments and savings.

He was slightly chubby, unlike Mum and, also unlike her, he was always very natural with us kids, playing fun games with us up in Paul's bedroom at weekends, out of Mum's way. He was also very tactile, again in complete contrast to my mother, who didn't show much affection. Dad would think nothing of giving us kisses and cuddles. He was my hero. No other daddy could ever match my daddy. I had the best in the world.

I also admired and adored my big brother. Paul wanted to be an astronaut when he grew up and I remember Dad making up a song about it that would have us all squealing with laughter.

'I have a little boy and Paul-Michael is his name. He wants to fly up into space upon a rocket plane. With Daniel by his side, through the galaxy they'll ride and they won't come back no more!'

This was typical Dad. He had a talent for words, and could make up rhymes effortlessly, cracking us up time and time again.

As for me, I was a happy little girl. I enjoyed school and had lots of friends.

It was a few years before then that my grandpa, my mum's dad, died. I don't really remember much about him, but I do know that Mum took his death very badly.

This was my first encounter with death and I was very confused by it. I knew from the TV that people who had died were buried in coffins, so I re-enacted a burial with a Barbie doll, putting her into a plastic box.

My mother saw me doing it and asked me what I was doing. I replied quite simply and innocently that I was putting her in her coffin because she was dead. My mother snapped, smacking me and insisting that I must never ever say such things again. This seemed to be an extreme reaction, even for my mother, as I battled to understand what I had actually done wrong.

At school, I would spend my time with my three best friends, Diane, Laura and Heather. Often after school I would go to play at Heather's house, riding up and down her street on her scooter. Her father had a gambling fruit machine in the front room, which I always thought was so 'cool'. It was something I knew you usually only found in pubs and clubs, and was for grown-ups. It emphasised how very different Heather's upbringing was from my own. There was fun in her house, and practically an open-door policy with friends coming and going. And that was a privilege I was most definitely not allowed.

On the one occasion, after I had nagged and nagged my mother to let me have a friend over to play, Laura came round. Laura was desperate to play my Care Bears tape in my bedroom but I wasn't so keen. One of the characters, Professor Coldheart, sang a song that scared me rigid about the Care Bears being locked up alone. That particular song made me feel so afraid and alone that the compassion I felt for those bears with no one to love them would overwhelm me. But my mother forced me to play the tape to Laura, and, distraught, I ran out of the room in tears. Needless to say, Laura never came over again. Mum never invited her, and Laura didn't ask to return.

I also played with Kay and Nicola, who lived just round the corner from my house. I have a vivid memory of watching the wedding of Prince Andrew and Sarah Ferguson at Kay's house. As I stared at Sarah on the screen, thinking how amazingly beautiful she was in her wedding dress, Kay's mother caught my eye and beckoned me to join her on the sofa while Kay and Nicola played. I snuggled up as close as I could, enjoying the cosy proximity in which we sat, breathing in her mummy scent. This felt like nothing I had ever experienced with my own mother. I didn't want the wedding to end. I didn't want to have to acknowledge that this was not my own mother cuddling me close. For those few hours, I felt what it was like to have a real mum.

But the reality was that, in general, my family was not very sociable. My parents had only one or two very good friends. Dad's best friend was 'Uncle Keith'. They had been at college together, and Keith was my godfather. Uncle Keith was single and very religious. He worked for the Church in Kent and always seemed calm and composed, with a voice so soft and gentle yet compelling that people would stop to listen to what he had to say.

Mum's friend was 'Auntie Shirley', who was married to 'Uncle Peter', also my godparents. They lived just close by near my school.

Auntie Shirley became very ill with leukaemia, something she kept to herself in the vain hope of sparing her friends and family grief. Her death came as a massive shock to both her husband and my mum. I don't think either of them ever really came to terms with the loss.

Having lost her dad and her best friend, my mother sank to her lowest point. From this time onwards she was on anti-depressants and relied solely on my father for his support, both emotionally and financially. We were terribly isolated. We lived in a large four-bedroomed semi-detached house but, despite the houses that surrounded us, we may as well have been living in the street alone. Nearby was a house belonging to another young family. They had a daughter called Emma, who had striking long blonde hair. Next door was a family with a young girl called Sara, but I was never encouraged to play with either of these girls. So,

I had my school friends while I was at school but I felt strangely alone at home.

In 1988, my parents made a decision that would change my life for ever. They decided to move to West Wales. I remember clearly the moment I was told. The idea of leaving all my friends and my life as I knew it felt unbearable. I couldn't comprehend it. There seemed to be no explanation for the move, no real reason behind it. To make matters worse, my parents must have delayed telling Paul and me of their decision, because no sooner did we know we were moving than we were off.

I did know and like West Wales, though, because we had spent many holidays in the seaside town of Cardigan. My parents had bought a plot of land in an idyllic village called Llechryd. A local builder was developing the site and they had become very involved in the design and layout of what was meant to be their dream home.

There was, they told me and my brother, a nice local school just a short walk across the village, where we would start after the summer holidays. It was almost too good to be true.

Since Grandpa had died and Nanna was all alone, she was to move with us to be nearer my mother, her only daughter. Nanna bought one of the plots on the same estate and the idea was that she would become a closer part of our family. I think my parents truly believed that once we moved into this perfect home we would become a happy family.

As we finally left Church End Lane and our car pulled out of the drive, we were all chanting, 'Goodbye, House!' and I remember wondering what might lie ahead. What friends would I make? What would the future hold for me? So many questions filled my mind as I sat in that car making the long journey to Wales. My life was about to change completely, and I had no idea where this new life would lead. That realisation both scared and excited me; it was the same sort of feeling I had when we were setting off on holiday. What would it be like? Would I have fun? Would I be happy? But this time the circumstances were different; this time I wasn't coming back.

2

Home Sweet Home

Five hours, two toilet stops, and one argument with Paul later, we arrived in West Wales. I had never seen so much rain in all my life. The sound reverberating off the windscreen was like a brass band; cymbals crashing with every thrash of rain. The move was not quite the picture of happiness my parents had envisaged. I sat quite smug at the thought that I was right: that moving would not be the perfect pathway to a happy family. I had wanted to stay with my friends and old life, and in the pouring rain felt sure that Mum and Dad would soon realise we were better off back in Essex.

As we pulled into the Glanarberth estate even I, at seven years old, could work out that a housing development was not meant to look like a muddy building site. There were cement mixers and piles of neatly stacked bricks where I supposed my bedroom should have been. The basic structure of the property was all that was visible. Things were not going at all to plan. Chaos was not something my mother had much time for. Her obsessive tendencies demanded order and precision at all times.

An eerie silence came over my parents and they seemed unable to close their mouths. Paul and I realised that it was best not to state the obvious. We sat quietly while a storm at least on a par with the one outside erupted inside our car.

'What the hell is going on, Mike?' came my mother's eventual question. Her tone suggested accusation.

'Wait here,' was his weary response.

A brief but very angry conversation followed between my parents as Dad parked and strode towards the on-site Portakabin.

Half an hour later he returned, grim-faced, and we drove towards a town a few miles from Llechryd called Newcastle Emlyn and checked into the Emlyn Arms Hotel.

This journey felt almost as long as the trip from Essex as my mum and dad desperately tried to rationalise how things could have ended up this way, and why they had not been informed of the building delays before they left Runwell.

I bit my tongue.

Almost as soon as we'd been shown to the hotel's family room my parents put me and my brother to bed so that they could discuss what they were going to do.

We were homeless. And this brought with it a whole new set of worries and concerns. It was bad enough moving to a new house and having to make new friends from scratch with the neighbours, but it was far worse to fetch up with no house and no neighbours. Some other girl was sleeping in my old room in Runwell and I had no room at all, and no idea what the next day would bring.

As I fell asleep I recalled the initial delight I had felt at my parents' misfortune and felt pangs of guilt. Serves me right, I thought, for wanting things to go wrong. I now understood the saying, 'Be careful what you wish for.'

The next morning I awoke to a clear sky and the sound of the kettle boiling as Dad made Mum a cup of tea. It was as though the bad weather of the night before had never existed and the slate had been wiped clean for a new day and new possibilities. Here was my chance to make amends, and I decided that perhaps living in Wales would not be so bad after all. The anxiety of being homeless had evolved into excitement. Where would we go? What would we do? It was an adventure.

My parents' long discussion the night before had

produced results. We were told to get dressed quickly. There were things to do and places to see.

The first point of call after breakfast was a little village between Newcastle Emlyn and Llechryd, called Cenarth. We visited the caravan park there, and my parents spent what seemed like hours discussing mundane issues with the site manager, looking inside and out. The manager recited prices, and eventually Mum and Dad decided that they would buy a static caravan (or, as my mum liked to call it, a 'mobile home') with the profit made from our Runwell house. Once this decision had been made, the atmosphere of stress and anxiety lifted and we spent the remainder of our time at the hotel anticipating our move to the caravan.

The weeks that followed are some of the happiest of my life. Living in that caravan was such an adventure. Paul and I had free run of the caravan site. We discovered a little path that ran down to a secluded part of the river, in reality a little stream, and Paul and I named it 'the Beach'. Every day was spent playing, bathing and fishing in the little stream. We made lots of new friends who were there on holiday and who found it fascinating that this was our home.

We left there after some time for Castle Malgwyn, a large hotel set back from the road, with a long drive leading up to its entrance. The grounds were large and beautiful, with an abundance of trees and shrubs and a swimming pool to the left of the building. The front exterior of the hotel was covered in ivy, and looked extremely impressive. Paul and I enjoyed calling this our 'home' and I felt like a princess, running through the hallways, exploring the different rooms.

Paul and I were enrolled at the local village school and my first day was something I shall never forget. I was used to being part of the furniture in my previous school and found it difficult to adjust to being 'the new girl'. I was shown into my classroom, and I remember looking around at the girls in my class, particularly paying attention to three named Felicity, Victoria and Emily, and hoping that they would be my friends. Indeed, they would come to have a huge influence on my life.

Two incidents stand out in those first weeks at school. We had to learn Welsh – a huge challenge for a seven-year-old who had never spoken a word of the language before now, and one that I struggled to meet. One day, our teacher, Mrs Osborne, read us a short-story extract in Welsh and then started asking questions. I hadn't the foggiest idea what the story had been about and was helpless to reply. The shame of those few seconds when the whole class was staring at me waiting for me to say something felt like an eternity. Turning a deep shade of purple, I hurriedly said that I needed the toilet and rushed to escape from the glares of the other children as quickly as my legs could carry me. As I walked through the school hall towards the girls' toilets, I noticed a sign in the cloakroom saying, 'Wet Paint – Do Not Touch!'. For some reason I just had to touch.

As I leaned over and put a fingertip to the paint there was a loud shout behind me that sent my heart into overdrive. I spun around to be confronted by a man decorating the school. I felt a warm trickle down my legs. The shame I had felt in class was now multiplied a hundred times. I mumbled my apologies and ran to the toilets where I cried and cried with shame and embarrassment.

I was too mortified to tell anyone what had happened and just dried my underwear and legs with toilet paper before bracing myself to return to class. At that moment the bell rang for break time and I thankfully filed outside with the other children, hoping that no one would notice me.

After a few weeks at the hotel, we moved into a rented cottage on a holiday-home site. I celebrated my eighth birthday while we were there and it was on my birthday that my father sat me down and decided that it was about time I learned to tell the time. He drew a large clock on a piece of paper, and went through the logistics of how a clock worked and the five times table. He persevered with me, and by the time I got up I could tell the time perfectly. That was typical of my relationship with my dad. He told me things in a way that I understood. I could never have imagined sitting down with my mum and learning how to tell the time without a big argument developing. My dad had the patience of a saint.

After a fourth temporary move, our house in Llechryd was finally ready for us and we gave Nanna the good news that her house was finished too and she could join us in Wales. I had desperately missed her and looked forward to seeing her and to getting into a routine again and having a room of my own. The night before the move, I lay unable to sleep, I was so excited. I laughed to myself about how much I had dreaded moving to Llechryd, and how completely different I now felt about it.

When I finally fell asleep, I dreamed the dream I had had for years countless times before.

I am standing on the clouds in a white dress, as a long rope ladder gently falls beside me. I climb up the ladder, going higher and higher into the clouds until I finally reach the top rung. I climb on to the cloud that is beside me, which is covered in beautiful pink and yellow flowers, which I sit picking contentedly, blissfully unaware of anything other than my surroundings . . .

I was completely unaware of the dream's meaning or symbolism, but had noticed that it would occur whenever I was feeling happy or settled.

That night was the last time that I would ever have that dream.

On the day of the move I had expected Mum to be as happy and excited as I was. I should have remembered that her moods were not something that could be easily predicted. As I grew older I understood that Mum's anxiety and depression were part of our daily lives and they were easier to live with if Paul and I kept out of her way and in her good books. So the day of the move we kept a low profile as we made the short drive to the Glanarberth estate.

It looked much more welcoming now, with its neat array of professional-looking bungalows. We soon discovered that they were occupied by either elderly or retired couples, and that we were the only young family there. It was a huge setback to me as I had imagined making lots of local friends. But I quickly learned that my three school friends all lived within walking distance, so my initial disappointment was short-lived.

Our large bungalow was called 'Morgeney', named by my parents after the stream that ran beneath the foundations. Nanna moved in a few days later to her property, 'Mwnt', named after the beach a few miles away.

From the moment that my mum had her own place again her behaviour changed dramatically. During the periods we had spent in temporary accommodation she hadn't seemed so over-anxious about the houses we lived in; now, though, she seemed to become completely obsessed with the cleanliness of the house and immediately imposed a lot of rules and regulations on Paul and me. We had no choice but to comply.

Each time we came home, we would have to knock on the door and wait for her to answer. It didn't matter that the door was unlocked or that we knew she was home. We were simply not allowed to enter until she said so. I remember the embarrassment of waiting there on the doorstep, wondering if the neighbours on the estate were watching this ridiculous routine.

When she had opened the door, we had to remove our shoes before entering the house and, once inside, we were forbidden to touch anything and had to go straight to the kitchen. Mum didn't want the perfection of her house spoiled in any way, although I often wondered what damage we could possibly cause by simply walking through the house. But to Mum, this edict was incredibly important and, as children, Paul and I felt helpless and unable to question her rules.

In the kitchen, we would have to position our school bags carefully on a special vinyl mat. Then, reaching for a tub of baby wipes that were kept within easy reach on the worktop, Mum would take our coats off, and 'clean' our hands and faces with the wipes before sending us off to the lounge.

None of us, not even my dad, was allowed to do simple tasks in the house such as making a drink or getting something to eat when hungry. We had to wait until Mum decided it was time to eat or drink. She ruled the entire household and we had to fit in around her.

This bizarre behaviour ruled our daily routine. We were not allowed to sit on the sofas or even up against them. They were reserved for Mum and Dad's use only, and Paul and I were only ever allowed to sit on the carpet. This was always extremely frustrating, especially when my back ached from the lack of support. So Paul and I would each grab the turtle footstool and attempt to lean against it as soon as our mother left the room. She had told us countless times not to do that, as apparently we would 'bend it out of shape', but as soon as her back was turned the rule would be broken in our attempts to relieve some small part of our unbearable lifestyle.

We would have to remain in the living room until we were told to move. Even a trip to the bathroom had to be requested and carried out only when Mum said it was a suitable time. After using the toilet, we would have to call Dad to come and wipe our bottoms as we were not allowed the privilege of wiping our own. I can't remember an occasion where Mum ever did this duty herself; however she tried not to have us home too often if she was alone, and I eventually spent the majority of my time with my nanna. The only times I was home, Dad would invariably be there too, hence all my memories of 'bottom wiping' involve my dad rather than my mum. The embarrassment was unbearable, especially if Dad was caught up with one of the endless tasks my mother had set him. We would have to wait on the toilet until he was free to come and see to us. I was now eight years old, and Paul was ten, so it seemed unreasonable to have to undergo such a humiliating experience. Yet again, however, we felt helplessly unable to object. Life in our household was one that was easier to bear if we kept quiet without causing any confrontation.

There wasn't a thing in the entire house that I had access to. Even the choice of my clothes was my mother's privilege. Each morning my clothes would be laid neatly on the floor in my room, ready for me to put on, after being organised the previous evening. That done, I would then have to leave my room for the entire day so that Mum could clean and tidy, ready for me to sleep there that evening.

My bedroom, far from being the personal space that I had longed for, became a show room once more. So much for the perfect existence moving to Wales was supposed to bring. I had hoped that now I was getting older I would have more freedom, especially in my own bedroom. However, I wasn't allowed to touch a single item of furniture. I longed to know what was in my chest of drawers and would sit daydreaming for hours about the possibilities. On the occasions that my mother opened my wardrobe when I was in the room, I would stare in fascination at the wonders within, desperate to get a glance and satisfy my curiosity. Obviously I had some idea of the clothes that I owned, but my wardrobe housed a section of three shelves that seemed full of gifts and trinkets that I had obviously been given over the years. Ironic, as they had never actually been given to me at all, Mum had obviously stashed these goodies away, desperate for me not to make a mess with them.

The bizarre consequence of this obsessive behaviour

was that I longed to be allowed to clean my room and make my own bed. Friends at school frequently complained about these tasks, but I secretly thought they were the luckiest children alive. I dreamed of the freedom to be able to put things in my room wherever I wanted them, and to have the responsibility of keeping it clean and tidy. When I asked Mum, she answered curtly. She wanted things done properly and so would do them herself.

Each evening, Paul and I would be called separately into the kitchen to undress ready for bed. We would have to take our clothes off and leave them in a pile on the floor, then put our nightclothes on. During this procedure Mum would make sure we didn't make any mess, and then wipe down our faces, hands and feet before sending us to the bathroom for my dad to brush our teeth. This routine never changed. We would stand in almost military fashion with our hands out in front of us, waiting to be cleaned. First our hands, then our faces. With quick strokes Mum would wipe away the imaginary dirt that she believed had contaminated us during the course of the day. Feet were the last part and the worst, as we had to stand on one leg for her to wipe the sole of each foot. This was especially hard as she didn't want us to hold on to anything in case we dirtied the spotless kitchen worktop. Night after night we would wobble as we desperately tried to balance on one leg, keen to leave the kitchen and have some time to ourselves.

Our thoughts were our only privacy. I used to yearn for bedtime so that I could think whatever thoughts took my fancy; these were the only things it seemed that weren't dictated during my childhood. Bed was the one place where I could escape my mother's restrictions.

The only person to whom the rules didn't apply was our dog, Katie. Katie was a little black Llhasa Apso whom we all adored.

She was a good-natured dog, and never seemed to tire of the constant pulling of her fur or being picked up by us kids. She had been bought from a family who mistreated her and so Mum had put a lot of time and effort when she first had her into rebuilding the trust in human kind that Katie so obviously lacked. Because of this, Katie and my mum were inseparable. Katie had her own chair in the living room at home, which was ironic as Paul and I were not allowed that privilege. She was even allowed to sleep in my parents' bed, lying between them, cuddled up to my mum. Her food was another luxury. Katie didn't eat standard tins of dog food; instead Mum cooked her fresh chicken and she ate only what the rest of the family ate.

Mum often showed more affection for the dog than she did to Paul and me. But I know that Mum cared deeply about us and I have no doubt in my mind that she really loved us. I believe that she was just coping with life as best as she could. Showing her emotions was not something that came naturally to her, but I never felt that we were in any way unloved.

But, apart from Katie, the rest of us had to abide by the rules. And that included my dad, who did the chores asked of him the moment Mum said they needed doing. Dad was never able just to sit and watch TV with Paul and me in the lounge. Dad had to be with Mum at all times and couldn't make his own choices or do anything for himself. He couldn't even take a shower when he wanted. Everything had to be run by Mum first. And he couldn't even sleep on his own pillow. Mum insisted on spreading a towel across his pillow-case, supposedly because, she said, he suffered from dandruff that would make the pillowcase dirty. He abided by the rules, just as we did, whether from a desire to keep her spirits high or because he was afraid to stand up against her, I will never know. But we never saw him complain.

I found the restrictions extremely difficult, and as a result spent as much time with my grandmother as I possibly could. She seemed to have a good relationship with my mum, although she was well aware of her obsessive tendencies. I think this contributed towards our closeness as she took me under her wing. Nanna had an obvious dislike for my dad. It was never something she mentioned or explained, but there were various arguments that would erupt, and Nanna would make her feelings towards my dad quite clear.

'Nan' became my mother figure and my time with her consisted of doing the things that I supposed other children of my age were able to do. Routine tasks such as helping her with her housework and assisting with the cooking gave me so much pleasure and delight, and an insight as to what a 'normal' life could be. Rather than causing me to resent my own mother and the life to which she subjected me, I simply grew to adore my nan, spending every evening, holiday and weekend with her.

She indulged my delight in cooking by allowing me to create little menus and then 'cook' the various dishes. She never once complained about the food I made. Every dish, she'd declare, was the 'best I had ever had', and her words filled me with pride and a sense of achievement. My nan and I were like best friends. And, initially, my mother seemed pleased about that. It gave her the space and time to continue with her household tasks, with one less person to think about.

Mum began leaving me at Nan's later and later each night, often until eleven o'clock. She didn't want me home, it seemed. Eventually my dad would be sent to collect me. But the neighbours began to comment. For a child in primary school, being up so late every evening with school the next day inevitably began to take its toll. Some days I felt so tired in school that I would feel my head begin to loll and I would jolt upright in the realisation that if I wasn't careful I would fall asleep in class. Nan herself even complained a few times that she thought I should be collected a little earlier. But she too appeared to fall under my mother's power, 'not wanting to upset the apple cart'.

After a while, however, my mother became jealous of the closeness Nan and I shared and she imposed restrictions on the amount of time that I spent with Nan at the weekends. Week nights, however, remained the same – rather than bringing me home earlier, which would have seemed more appropriate. Mum decided that I should spend every Saturday at home with her and Dad, and it was Paul who was allowed to visit Nan on his own. This filled me with a sense of dread. I knew my weekend routine would now consist of shopping on a Saturday morning, followed by afternoons in front of the TV on the floor while Mum and Dad 'sorted out the house'. I would much rather have spent the time with my nan. At her house I could at least have a normal existence.

This new arrangement changed my life for ever. Here, at the age of eight, the downward spiral that would dictate my life began. Sometimes I wonder if my mother knew what she was letting herself in for when she made the decision to bring me closer into the family unit. She ended up locking me out of family life forever.

3

Daddy's Little Girl

On a typical Saturday morning I would be woken up by my dad, eat breakfast and get dressed, then sit in the lounge waiting for my mother to complete whatever chores she felt compelled to complete, before she was ready to leave the house to do the weekly shop.

In the supermarket we would wander up and down the aisles while Mum decided which products would meet her exacting standards. When we got home, my dad and I would have to wait in the car to give Mum the time she needed to unpack the shopping. This involved her cleaning each package with baby wipes before putting it away – a process that could easily take up to two hours and was undertaken every time we went shopping. She would indicate when she was ready for us to go inside by appearing in the doorway and beckoning for us to enter the property.

This was how I quickly came to regard our house; to me it was merely a property and not a home. A home evoked to me the idea of feelings of warmth and happiness, things that I certainly didn't feel here. The temporary places we had lived in had felt more homely than Morgeney, despite the embroidered 'Home Sweet Home' that Mum had hung in the kitchen.

One Saturday, after all the shopping and putting-away, I remember sitting on my dad's lap in the dining area of our open-plan kitchen while Mum made a salad for lunch. I suddenly became aware of Dad's hand between my legs. I immediately edged away, feeling distinctly uncomfortable. My reaction was to voice my incomprehension at what had happened.

I called out, 'Mum? Dad just touched my bum.' At eight, I had no words to describe the difference between the vaginal and anal areas.

The reaction I received would set the pattern for years to come and cloud my judgement. Dad piped up, 'No, I didn't!' and Mum's response was, 'Don't be so ridiculous, Julia!'

I remember sitting there contemplating the responses I had been given. Mum and Dad's conversation had quickly moved on to other things and I concluded that such topics were not to be discussed. It was a lesson I would never forget. I knew full well that my father had lied to my mum. At the same time I couldn't help doubting myself when he denied it had happened. The inner turmoil I felt for that moment was so confusing, I couldn't think clearly what was the truth. I was torn between the realisation that my dad had lied to my mum, and that he had touched me.

I decided, irrespective of who had said what, that it was unlikely ever to happen again, and I satisfied myself with this explanation, allowing myself mentally to pick up the fragments of my parents' conversation.

I didn't think any more of the incident until a week later, when we went shopping again. As usual on our return home, Dad dropped the shopping bags off with Mum at the door, then sat in the car with me while we waited to be called.

I was allowed to climb into the front seat to sit with Dad and listen to his Neil Sedaka and Gene Pitney tapes. I loved the freedom of singing along in the front with my dad without my mum there to tell us to turn the music down.

But this time, as I sprawled out across the front seat, feet up on the dashboard in a blissful act of rebellion, Dad's hand wandered again. He placed his hand on my leg, slowly moving it up my skirt. I sat rigid, completely unsure of what to do.

The previous week in the kitchen came back to me, and I remembered his reaction when I had told Mum what he had done. It would be pointless, I reasoned, waiting until we got inside to tell Mum about being touched again, as the same thing would happen. I understood this, and so felt completely powerless. I thought that Dad must be cross with me for telling Mum the last time it had happened, and so this would have to be kept a secret between Dad and me.

The only way I could cope was to block out what was happening. I just sat there, still, and thought that if I didn't mention it and didn't give it solidity by talking about it, then maybe it wasn't real, wasn't really happening. This innocent rationalising was the only way I could somehow comprehend what was happening to me.

Dad's hand continued exploring up my skirt, and he rubbed his fingers against the outside of my knickers.

I don't think I have ever felt as confused as I did at that moment, before or since. Dad was the only person in my life, other than my nan, who had ever shown me any warmth or tenderness. Dad was the one I could talk to, the one I could trust. So surely this couldn't be a bad thing? Was this just something that dads did to their daughters? I had so many questions. But it wasn't until Mum's face appeared at the window at the front of the house as she put some things away in her bedroom that I got an answer. Dad's reaction to seeing her told me what I needed to know. He instantly pulled away from me, withdrawing his hand guiltily at the prospect of being caught, saying, 'Quick – it's your mother.' It was obvious then to me that this was a 'secret'. Our secret. This was definitely something Mum was not supposed to learn about and, knowing her, I certainly didn't want to give her any reason to be cross with me. Mum never hurt us physically, but she could be very vicious verbally. Upsetting her always resulted in a fierce telling-off from both her and Dad, and was something we avoided at all costs.

I decided there and then that I would never mention to anyone what had happened, as it must surely be something that I had done wrong. I had, after all, let it happen. I knew I should probably say something, say no, but I loved my dad and didn't want to hurt his feelings. But this, I felt, made me as guilty as he was.

Dad's 'touching' became a frequent occurrence. Every Saturday after shopping we would sit in the car and his hand would venture between my legs. I would sit there just waiting for it, knowing that it would happen again. And every Saturday I was right.

Dad would initially put his hand on my leg as I sat still, switching off mentally. Somehow I developed the ability to think of other things while it was going on. I would daydream about school and continue singing along to the likes of Gene Pitney in my head almost as though this was normal. The oddest thing is that it did soon become normal.

Dad soon graduated from just putting his hand on top of my knickers to slipping his fingers inside. I still felt powerless to stop him. This was my dad and I adored him. I didn't know how else to cope with the situation apart from pretending it simply wasn't happening.

In the utmost betrayal and contamination of my innocence, Dad would use these opportunities not only to satisfy his own sexual needs, but to attempt to stimulate my own. He would rub his fingers along my vulva, flicking his fingertips over my clitoris. At such a young age, I didn't even know what a clitoris was, but I knew that when he touched me down there, it felt 'funny'.

I felt shame and humiliation that my father was touching me, but I also felt guilt and embarrassment that he could succeed in making me feel 'wet' between my legs – a sensation to which I was not accustomed. I felt guilty and confused as to why the wetness was there. I used to panic, thinking that Dad would be disgusted with me for being so dirty, but he never seemed to mind.

These confusing and conflicting emotions are the

most traumatic consequence of sexual abuse. As a little girl I could not comprehend the involuntary sensations produced when he touched me. The feelings of guilt and shame turned to self-loathing. I would feel so dirty afterwards, and hate myself for letting it feel OK. I didn't understand that this was my body's natural reaction, and one that I could not control. It is this ultimate betrayal that stops an abused child from speaking out and keeps secrecy levels high.

If Dad had ever hurt me or been aggressive, I think I would have found coping with his behaviour much easier. At times, when the touching first began, I thought it was fun. I was eight. I would beckon Dad into my room at night to play, and even encourage him to do things. I now know that this is the way in which abusers groom their prey, building up trust and a feeling of security. False security, of course. Thanks to my silence and complicity, Dad grew in confidence. He began chatting with me during these 'sessions'. After a number of weeks of me saying nothing to Mum, I suppose he concluded that this would indeed be our little secret and so took steps to reassure me that what was happening was perfectly normal for girls when they were growing up. He talked about how he had done things with a girl who lived nearby and that this was all OK. This seemed to answer my concerns about why this was happening to me. He seemed to be saying that it happened to lots of girls. And I assumed that all girls kept this secret from their mums. But the one thing that didn't make sense was that it continued to feel so wrong. Although I still felt utterly confused, I now at least knew that I wasn't alone and that this happened to other people too.

Dad kept on telling me how much he loved me and asked me to sit on his lap so he could kiss me. I thought it would be an 'adult kiss', which I assumed, was just a kiss that lasted for ages with your lips together.

When he put his tongue inside my mouth I was horrified. I didn't know what to do. Not wanting to upset Dad or make him angry with me was always a key factor. I didn't want to lose my dad by doing the wrong thing. He was the only parent that I felt close to, so I let him 'kiss' me in this way. But I thought how disgusting it was, and felt horrified that adults actually did this kind of thing. My disdain must have been apparent, as my dad didn't ever try to kiss me like that again.

He continued to try to make the situation 'normal'. He would try to make what he was doing into a game, and encouraged me to touch him as well as him touching me as part of the game. One game we would play involved him touching me somewhere, and then I would have to copy and touch him back in the same place. The game would begin quite innocently. He would touch my arm or leg and then I would touch his. But as time went on he would progress to touching me between my legs and wait for me to return the touch. If he touched me beneath my clothes, he would comment that I was cheating if I simply brushed against him on top of his clothes. He began opening his trousers so that I could see his 'willy', as I called it then. He would encourage me to touch it and showed me, with his hand on top of mine, how he liked it rubbed up and down. I was very nervous, very afraid of hurting his feelings or upsetting him if I refused to do anything he asked. I tried to keep him happy, but inside I was battling with my own feelings of guilt and shame that this was happening. I felt very dirty and so powerless to do anything about it.

Living with Dad became extremely difficult. I didn't know how to look at him any longer. He would behave very inappropriately towards me in the house, but was always careful not to make it apparent to Mum or Paul. He had a certain smile when he looked at me and I would notice him brushing past me, or assessing approvingly the things I wore, which always made me feel uncomfortable. At night, I would call him to bring me a drink in bed, and he would stand in my bedroom and pull his willy through the gap in his pyjama trousers and ask me to touch it. He could never stay long in my room as Mum was always around; so at least in the house I had some place of respite.

The burden of it all began to show itself physically. I began vomiting daily, and no one knew why. I couldn't explain why I felt so sick, or why the sickness just never seemed to go away. I was permanently nauseous. At the time I was unable to make the connection between the sickness and the abuse, and assumed that there must be something physically wrong with me, as Mum and Dad seemed convinced there must be. They took me to the GP, who referred me to the hospital for some tests. I had to undergo a barium meal, which involved me drinking a chalky-tasting drink whilst my insides were X-rayed. But despite this and various rather medical tests and procedures, no one was able to find a cause for my persistent sickness, and it was eventually put down to 'stomach migraines'.

Why was a child of eight or nine presenting such symptoms? Surely someone should have investigated my symptoms further. But no further investigations were instigated and I was left to continue with the double life that I had become used to enduring. I felt as though I was two people: the child and daughter, and the girl who had a terrible secret that no one could ever find out. I sincerely believed that if anyone ever knew I would be in a lot of trouble and would lose the family I had around me. At such a young age that option was something I couldn't begin to contemplate.

The thing that I found the hardest to understand was that, Dad's 'games' in the car aside, life carried on as normal. I continued going to school, seeing as much of my nan as I could, and playing with Felicity, Vicky and Emily. My life had taken a dramatic turn, yet everything around me continued as it ever had. Nothing else changed at all. And then the news came that a baby was on the way.

4
Smartie Tube

The day that Mum and Dad told me that they were having another baby I had been playing up all day. I was nine, a difficult age. I was desperately trying to gain some independence and find myself, and this was particularly difficult given the restrictions my mother imposed.

On hearing the news, I was absolutely elated. I had been nagging for ages that I'd love to have a baby in the house and this news was like a light finally being switched on in my life.

I had felt so down and unhappy, coping alone with the terrible secret in my life, that the thought of a baby gave me a whole new perspective. I would lie awake for hours dreaming up names and wondering whether I would have another brother or a little sister. The pregnancy brought me and Mum closer together. Her revelation had given us some common ground and I could have happily chatted to her about the new arrival all day long.

Each morning, I would get into Mum's bed when Dad got up to make breakfast and I'd lie next to her with the latest additions to the list of the baby's names. It goes without saying that I would have to ensure I lay on the towel put over Dad's pillow, but I didn't mind this rule as long as my little brother or sister was there with us as we talked.

Life was changing, but the abuse continued. Mum's pregnancy didn't seem to make any difference to Dad whatsoever, and I soon learned from their rows that this pregnancy was not planned as far as my father was concerned. He seemed to feel that he was past his child-rearing years and was content with the two children he had already. This argument continued throughout the pregnancy although Dad seemed to come to terms with the prospect of another child shortly before the birth.

The baby was delivered by Caesarean section on 26 November 1990. We knew the baby was going to be a boy – a little brother. Andrew was the most beautiful little thing I had ever seen in my life. I fell in love with him instantly and relished every moment I had with him. I felt almost as though he was my own son, and I delighted at every new noise and movement he made.

I think I had imagined that a new baby in the house would somehow alter my dad's pattern of repeated abuse that I had been subjected to for almost two years now. On the contrary, after Andrew's birth he upped the pace, seemingly no longer satisfied with just touching and game-playing.

I was ten. And as I began to develop breasts, Mum started buying me crop tops in place of the vests that I had previously worn. Crop tops were the cool thing to wear and most of the girls in my year at school had made this transition. During the times alone with Dad in the car, he would put his hand inside my crop top, and fondle my practically non-existent breasts in addition to touching me between the legs. He also began to play with himself a lot more and would rub his willy whilst playing with my genitals.

One day in the car, after another shopping trip, he was rubbing his willy as usual. I remember not knowing where to look or what to do with myself while he continued, and he leaned down into the side compartment of the door extracting a J-cloth that he kept for cleaning the windscreen. Dad continued rubbing himself and asked me to watch whilst he moved his hand up and down, gaining pace until a milky substance appeared on to the cloth as he groaned in pleasure. I stared in amazement as I tried to work out what this substance may be. At ten, my concept of sex was simply that a man put his willy into a woman's vagina and they moved around a bit. I had no comprehension of orgasms or ejaculation, and pondered over what I had just seen. Dad zipped up his trousers and went to dispose of the evidence.

In school I would listen intently when the other girls started to talk about sex, hoping to be able to piece together what I had seen to make some sense of it. Understandably the things that I had seen never came up in conversation and, obviously not wanting to draw any attention to myself, I never dared to ask.

This period was a difficult one. It was the norm to discuss such subjects; the other girls couldn't wait to get their first bras or start their periods, and many had their first boyfriends, playing 'kiss chase' in the school yard at break times. I would try to join in and be part of their discussions, desperately wanting to be one of them, but my concept of sex and puberty was one so different from their own that I didn't know how to communicate. I knew far more than they seemed to, which left me confused as to how much to say without causing suspicion.

In my secret life, Dad would continue to look for any opportunity for us to be alone together. He would sink so low as to use the fact that Mum was busy with the baby to get me by myself. Even when Mum was in hospital, just days after undergoing the major surgery of Andrew's delivery, Dad would stop the car on the way home from visiting her in order to touch me again. He would pull the car into the side of the road and fondle me before taking me back to Nan's, where both Paul and I were staying until Mum came home.

Before Andrew was born, Dad used to tell me that we would have lots of time together when Mum was in hospital and that I could sleep in his bed with him. This prospect terrified me as things were already progressing at a rate that completely overwhelmed me. It had been easier to switch off when it had been touching each other over clothes, but the intensity of the abuse, especially underneath my clothes, and watching him perform acts in front of me, left me feeling quite afraid of what might be next. I was frightened of what he would do if I slept in his bed. Scared that he would take things further on from the touching I had endured, afraid that he might want to do something else, something new, that I wouldn't know how to handle. I had no idea or comprehension of what that may be, but the fear of the unknown terrified me. Thankfully, though, Mum arranged for both Paul and me to be at Nan's for the duration of her hospital stay and I was never more thankful for the refuge of Nan's house. She had become my saviour once more.

Maybe from frustration at missing a prime chance or from a perverse need to take his fantasies further, Dad ensured that another opportunity quickly arose when we'd be undisturbed. One day, not long after Mum had come out of hospital, she was completely exhausted and stressed out. She'd already sent Paul to Nan's, the baby was sleeping, but I still needed watching. She shouted at Dad to take me out to give her some time to get through the household chores, and so Dad and I went to the park in Boncath, three or four miles away.

In Boncath, we played on the swings and slides but Dad also wanted to chat to me, so we walked around the grass while he talked. I can't remember what he said but I know how uncomfortable it made me feel, and the topic was most definitely sexual.

On returning to the car, Dad continued chatting to me, then asked me if I had ever had sex before.

I immediately thought what a stupid question he had asked. I was ten years old and didn't even really know what sex was so I simply replied, 'No.'

He then asked, 'Would you like to?'

I didn't know how to answer. I knew exactly where this conversation was leading and I couldn't find the words to handle it. I just sat there, as heavy as stone. I seemed to have lost the ability to function. I didn't know how to think rationally, feel or even move. Millions of thoughts were running through my head. What should I say? What would happen if I said no? What would happen if I said yes? What did he want me to say? The overwhelming desire was not to upset my dad. I was so scared of hurting his feelings, or making him cross with me, that I didn't know what to do. At the same time I couldn't make myself actually say 'yes'. I didn't want him to think that I actively wanted to do as he had asked, that I was making it happen. The only response I could find was, 'I don't mind.'

This seemed to satisfy him, and he immediately told me to take off my knickers and sit on his lap.

My heart was beating hard and fast as, with trembling hands, I pulled down my knickers, easing them over my shoes, and leaving them in a crumpled heap on the floor of the car. I just sat there looking straight ahead as he once more asked me to sit on his lap, explaining the logistics of how he wanted me to sit. He told me to climb on top of him and sit on his lap facing him with my legs on either side of him. The same position he had sat me in when he had kissed me that day.

I sat there a moment, looking straight ahead, listening to his words, hardly able to comprehend what I was hearing. Eventually I looked over, and noticed that he had already undone his trousers and was rubbing his hand up and down over his willy. I climbed over as he had asked and sat on his lap. Dad put his hand between my legs and began rubbing me with his fingers on my naked genitals. He then proceeded to try to push his willy inside my vagina. He asked if I was OK. I simply nodded, and he continued to try to enter me. After a few moments, he realised that he couldn't do it; he was unable to penetrate me.

Giving up, he told me to sit back on my seat, concluding that we would have to try again when I was a little 'older'. Thankfully, I accepted this escape and sat back down on my seat, scrambling on the floor for my knickers as my cheeks blazed with the shame and embarrassment of what had just happened.

Dad then tried to satisfy his perversions another way and asked me if I'd like to 'suck it' instead, indicating his exposed willy.

I was horrified. Why on earth would I want to suck it? Did people really do that, or was it some new game that Dad had made up? However much I didn't want to hurt Dad's feelings, however much I loved him, this was definitely not something I was prepared to do. The very thought of it made me feel as sick as if he had asked me to eat a slug. He persisted, saying, 'Well?' in a questioning manner. I battled inside with the best way to say no, and eventually muttered, 'Not this time.' I didn't know what else to say. Dad still wouldn't let it drop, obviously keen to change my mind, asking me, 'Why not?' My cheeks blazed red once more; I didn't know how to answer his question. I eventually answered dismissively, 'We have to save something for another time.' I was so desperate to keep him happy without compromising my decision not to do as he had asked. I hoped 'another time' would never come. I didn't think he would be cross, or punish me in any way, I just thought I would hurt his feelings. I didn't want him to be disappointed in me. I couldn't risk losing the love and affection of the only parent who had showed it to me.

Dad continued talking about how he wanted us to try to have sex again and came up with some suggestions that he thought might make things a little easier.

He told me that he wanted me to start 'preparing myself' so that things would not be as difficult next time. He wanted me to begin practising when I was in bed at night by inserting fingers inside myself, starting with one and working my way up to three. He asked me to tell him when I could manage three fingers inside me and then he would be able to try to have sex again.

I just sat there listening to his suggestions, not quite able to take in what he was asking me to do. I wondered whether I had heard him correctly, or maybe misinterpreted what he was saying. I kept waiting for him to say, 'Oh, come on – I'm only joking!' but the words never came. Dad really was serious about what he wanted me to do and he had every intention of trying to have sex with me again. I was petrified that if I ignored his instructions then he would notice when he tried again and would be cross with me for not doing as he asked. Even though Dad was always kind and gentle with anything he did to me, I didn't want to upset him for fear of what the consequences might be.

One night, as I lay in bed, I thought about the requests Dad had made and tried to do as he had asked in case he checked up on me any time soon. I attempted to insert just one finger inside myself. As soon as I felt the first pain I aborted the attempt. I felt an absolute failure, the most disgusting girl alive, so dirty that I hated myself for what was happening to me and what Dad had driven me to do. I felt scared of what reaction I might get when Dad realised that I couldn't do what he had asked of me, and dreaded the time when he would find out.

As these thoughts played in my head, I felt tears prickling inside my tightly shut eyelids. I couldn't hide from this any longer. My coping mechanism until now had been to ignore what was going on, blanking out most of it to the best of my ability. This was the first time that I had allowed myself truly to believe and try to make sense of what was happening to me.

Now I didn't know how to cope with the feelings I had any longer.

Part of me felt like it was my own fault. I had let all these things happen. I had never said no apart from the request to suck his willy. Maybe if I had refused to allow anything right from the start, this nightmare would never have even begun. I felt responsible for allowing things to get this far, but still helpless to do anything about it. My confusion was indescribable.

I loved my dad; I had always been close to him. He doted on me. So why was he doing this? What would Mum say if she knew?

I felt sure that the whole family would be torn apart if I told her, and that was only if she believed me. I suspected that she would instead believe that I had made the whole thing up, as she had that time in the kitchen, and then Dad would be cross with me for breaking our secret. I didn't feel as though I had a way out.

My head was swimming. Tears ran down my face, saturating the duvet as I squeezed it to my body. I lay as quietly as I could manage, petrified that Mum or Dad would hear my crying, discover the state I was in and demand an explanation. My body shook as I tried to contain my sobs.

At that moment the pain, the anger, the deceit, the

love, the sadness all compacted together. I felt as though I couldn't breathe, encompassed in this restrictive shell, unable to move. All these different emotions I childishly imagined were like Smarties packed together in a tube. The different colours represented every emotion that I felt. I was locked in a world of contrasting feelings, just waiting for the next time the tube would be opened and another emotion eaten away. As I fell into a troubled sleep, I wondered what would happen when the tube was finally empty.

5
Who Am I?

After this outburst, I tried my best not to allow myself to think any more about stopping the abuse. I told myself that there was no way out and that there was nothing I could do to solve my problems. I had to accept that the abuse and constant sickness were just a part of my life now, although I still didn't see a correlation between the two. As far as I was concerned, the sickness was merely another issue to contend with in an already hectic and turbulent life. I resolved to carry on as best as I could.

Despite everything, if I just concentrated on living from day to day, I could cope. This was my daily routine:

After school every day, I would go straight round to Nan's. Mum, Paul and Andrew would arrive later and stay for tea. Then, they would return home, leaving me with Nan until it was time for me to be collected by Dad to go home to bed.

It was a routine I loved. I would go to Nan's and watch kids' telly until five o'clock, then I would get the tea ready with my nan, and I really enjoyed helping to make sandwiches and cut up slices of cake for us all to eat.

Mum would bring our dog, Katie, along, cuddle up with her, and then ask us how our day had been and what work we had done at school. Despite Mum's efforts, all I ever wanted to do was watch TV, so I often ignored her attempts to chat about my day.

One day in particular, I was watching a programme called *Press Gang*. I sat glued to the screen, unable to believe my eyes as a story unfolded that was almost identical to my own. Paul had gone home – he had been bought a computer for his room, which he was allowed access to – but Mum was still in the room, chatting away in the background to my nan. I remember cringing; desperately trying to listen to the story, yet praying that my mum couldn't see or hear what was happening and my reaction to it. She seemed oblivious. I couldn't believe that there was a term for what was happening to me: 'sexual abuse'. I repeated those words again and again inside my head. Knowing there was a name for it was an immediate help. The confusion began to lift. It gave what Dad had been doing some solidity. And, as I watched the reactions of the people around the girl in this programme, the severity of what had been going on these past two years suddenly dawned on me.

People were outraged for her. They were furious. But, most of all, they kept saying how *it wasn't her fault*. Hearing those words was the big thing for me. Everything I was watching felt as though it was in some way intended for me – just me. I absorbed everything the girl was told and the realisation grew that I had to do something about my situation. It couldn't go on any longer. I didn't have to live this way.

That evening after tea, my friend Felicity came over to play in my nan's garden. Mum was still inside, chatting away with my nan before returning home to her endless chores. I wasn't allowed to have Felicity in the house, but we were quite happy exploring outdoors and running around without the watchful eye of a parent. Although my nan was much easier going than my mum, she still had certain rules and regulations, and not being allowed friends over was one of these. As Felicity and I played, I decided to break my silence and reveal the secret I had carried for two years.

I began tentatively, testing the water as to how she would react. I mentioned *Press Gang* and chatted about the storyline I had seen, about what had happened between this girl and her dad.

Felicity's response was encouraging. She said, 'Wouldn't it be awful if it happened to someone we know?'

This was my chance at last. If I was going to unburden myself, here was my cue to do it.

'It already has,' I said.

Felicity stared at me in disbelief.

'Who? Who has it happened to?'

I looked down at the gravel I was kicking around with my feet, tense and scared. Would she believe me? Was I doing the right thing?

'Me,' I replied.

Felicity was the first person I had told this secret to, the only person I had felt able to trust. I felt at that moment as bare and exposed as I had ever felt. She held in her hands the power to save or destroy me. I had shared something with her that I was relieved to have let go of, but I feared her reaction, and my stomach twisted into knots.

Fliss didn't let me down. She flung her arms around me and held me so tight I could feel the relief being released from my body. I sobbed and clung to her as though I could collapse at any second.

We talked for ages as I confided in her the reality of my double life. She never once interrupted, or offered her thoughts or opinion. Fliss simply took in everything

I was desperate to tell her. Now that I had opened these floodgates, I felt as though I would never be able to stop. Words were spilling uncontrollably out of my mouth.

When I had exhausted every aspect of my story, Fliss turned to me. 'Julia, I have a suggestion,' she said. 'You can say no if you like, and I won't mind, but why don't you come and talk to my mum? She would know what to say, and what you can do.'

After a moment's thought I decided that, having taken this first step, I couldn't stop now. I agreed that I would speak to her mum.

At that moment Nan began calling me in. It was starting to get dark. I hurriedly told Fliss that we would have to arrange for me to go over to her house to play, and she was not to mention my secret to anyone other than her mum.

I rushed inside, scared that my family would somehow know what I had just done, that they would be able to read it on my face. I sat down and tried not to look anyone in the eye. But Mum and Nan carried on as normal.

After Mum had gone home, I contemplated talking to my nan. We had the rest of the evening alone together. But somehow, even the closeness we shared couldn't stretch to my confessing my secret to her. I loved my nan, but I recognised that she was typically old-fashioned and prudish in her ways. I didn't feel able to find the words to explain to her what had been happening to me, although her dislike of my father had always been apparent to me. I knew also that she wouldn't want to rock the boat, and there was always the chance that she wouldn't believe me. Fear and embarrassment ensured I kept my silence.

That night, at eleven o'clock as usual, Dad came to collect me. I was thankful that the journey was only a short drive down the hill to our house, as I was sure that he would notice something was wrong.

I felt strangely guilty, as though I had let him down. I had broken an unspoken pact and hadn't remained loyal. Despite what was happening, I still loved my dad.

The next day, Felicity's mum, Mandy, called my mum, and asked if I could go for tea at their house the following day after school. Mum agreed and I began to look forward to seeing Mandy. I naïvely thought that she would come up with a solution that would solve everything, without anyone getting upset or knowing I had told anyone.

The day of the visit, I spent my time in school just staring at the blackboard. My mind kept drifting off, imagining all the different scenarios that could possibly present themselves that evening.

Finally the bell went for home time, and we headed

off to Fliss's house with her mum. Dinner was a Spanish omelette. It would make a reappearance later that night in a nervous episode of my so-called 'stomach migraines'.

After dinner, Mandy suggested I talk to her and her partner, Jan. I followed Mandy into the front room, where she sat me down and said that Felicity had told her some things that I had said about my dad, and would I like to tell her myself what had been going on.

Petrified, I began. Talking very slowly I managed to get the majority of the story out. Mandy and Jan remained supportive throughout, and said that they would help me; that it wasn't my fault. They never once doubted me, or assumed I had made it up. And that gave me the emotional support and reassurance that I so desperately needed. They asked if I would like to come over to play with Fliss another day that week, and agreed to ask my mum. After the chat I went back upstairs with Fliss and we played until it was time for me to go home.

Mandy and Jan remained downstairs to discuss what I had told them. I had no idea what they were saying, but I felt relieved finally to have grown-ups involved. With all the support I was receiving I was beginning to feel a little stronger and thought that maybe things wouldn't be so bad from now on. I sincerely believed that Mandy and Jan could fix this situation for me in some magical way. They had promised that they would help me, but I never once stopped to think about what kind of help it would be. I never once thought realistically about what could happen next.

A day or two later, as promised, Mandy arranged for me to go over to play with Fliss and I assumed that we'd have another chat before I went home. But this time, Mandy asked if I would like to go into town with them.

I sat in the back of their car chatting away with Fliss and honestly – naïvely – believed that we were going shopping. When we got to town, we walked towards an office building. Mandy turned to me and said that there were some people inside that she wanted me to meet, that they would be able to give me the help she had talked about, and that all I needed to do was tell them exactly what I had told her.

I started to panic. Where was I going? Who was I going to see? I knew it was too late to back out. I felt as though things were spiralling out of my control but decided that I would just have to do as she said, tell them – whoever they were – the truth, and then see if they could make things better for me. I held Fliss's hand tightly. She looked as nervous as I felt.

Inside, Fliss was shown to a play area. Mandy, Jan

and I were shown to a room. Two women sat waiting for us.

They were nice enough on first impressions and, full of smiles for me, introduced themselves as a social worker and a policewoman. That's when I really started to panic. Why were the police here? Why did they want to talk to me? Was I in trouble? Were they going to tell my parents? Suddenly I felt way out of my depth and just wanted to go away and forget the whole business.

But the social worker and policewoman did all they could to make me feel at ease, asking me a series of questions so that I didn't have to repeat my story all over again. I only had to elaborate where necessary to give a clearer picture as to what had been happening at home.

Everything I said was written down and at the end, an hour or so later, they asked me to sign the bottom of the paper to say that I confirmed everything I had said. I remember finding it really strange being asked to sign my name, and wondered for a moment whether they in fact wanted me to just write 'Julia', or whether I had to write my surname as well. I decided it was better to be safe than sorry and signed my whole name in my childlike scrawl across the bottom of the paper.

The social worker asked me if I had any questions. Now that I had calmed down a little, I mustered the courage to ask what had been on my lips for the entire interview.

'Are you going to tell my parents?'

After a pause, she replied, 'Yes. We have to.'

My stomach dropped.

I had conned myself into believing that this could all stay between the people in that room, that Mum and Dad would never have to find out what I had said. Now I knew that my whole life was about to change. How could I go home and live with Dad once he knew I had told someone our secret? What would happen to him? What would happen to me? What would Mum say? Would she believe me?

I had so many questions, but I knew these two women couldn't answer any of them for me.

I sat ashen-faced and simply shook my head when they asked if there was anything else I wanted to know. I didn't want to know any more, I only wanted to retreat back inside myself and ignore what was going on around me. I'd felt safer when I was in control of the secret. Now, somehow it felt that it would have been easier to let the abuse carry on. I could at least predict that. I knew what was coming, and what I needed to do to make Dad happy. Right then, I felt lost and out of control.

I can't remember a thing about the journey home. I

can't even remember if I went back to Fliss's house before Mandy took me back to Mum and Dad, or whether Dad came to collect me. The next few hours are a blur in my mind. I think I must have gone into shock. All I remember is that I somehow ended up at my nan's, sitting there on the sofa knowing what I'd done, but feeling too scared to warn or prepare her for the consequences.

I knew that fireworks were about to explode, but I didn't know what was going to happen or when. Suddenly my life had become muddled again. I now had three strands to it: my normal life, as my mother saw it; my secret life with Dad; and a further secret shared with Mandy and Jan that was about to emerge. The new uncertainty scared me. Something big was going to happen and it was entirely beyond my control.

Who was I in this whole mess? Where did I fit in? Where would my place be after this had all come out into the open? Which girl would I end up being? The confusion was indescribable, and it wouldn't be long before I found out.

6
I'm Sorry

It was Friday night. I was at Nan's waiting for the eleven o'clock deadline when Dad would come to collect me. But before that time arrived, the nightmare began to unfold.

Nan suddenly stared out of the window. Something had caught her eye. She exclaimed, 'Oh, goodness, a police car just went down the hill.'

This was unusual. We lived in an affluent area and my parents were the youngest homeowners on the estate. There was never any trouble, so the sight of a police car drew attention. I sat on the sofa and closed my eyes, praying that it was nothing to do with me.

Nan was up out of her chair in seconds, her watchful eye following the car's journey.

'Oh, my God, it's at your house!' she cried out.

My heart sank. I had known it would be connected with me. It felt just as bad, if not worse, as I had imagined it would feel.

I was petrified.

I have no recollection at all of what happened next. I can't remember if I said anything or gave Nan any indication that something awful was about to happen, but before I knew it, the phone rang. Nan ran to answer it and, needless to say, it was Mum. Nan took the call on the phone in her bedroom while I sat in the lounge, too scared to move. Usually, I would have been lurking outside her room, eager to catch a snippet of their conversation, but today I didn't want to know. The longer I could remain in ignorant bliss, the better.

I had no idea what they were saying, but assumed they would be really angry with me. I felt so responsible. Suddenly, the fact that everyone had been telling me it wasn't my fault didn't register any more.

Eventually Mum asked to speak to me. I took the phone from Nan with shaking hands and said with a trembling voice, 'Hello?'

Mum was in floods of tears. I had never heard her that upset before. I felt so guilty. I wanted to make everything better again but I didn't know how. My mother's words gave me something to think about.

'Julia, please tell me, if this did happen, then OK, don't worry about it, but if it didn't, then please, please tell me, this will all go away and Dad will come home again. This need never be mentioned again and no one will ever be cross with you.'

Suddenly, that idea sounded so appealing. I was being given a way out. I had an opportunity to make things better. I toyed with the idea for what then seemed an eternity but in reality was only a few seconds. I could make Dad not hate me if I took it all back. Mum would stop crying. My nan's worried expression would disappear and, like Mum had just said, no one would be cross with me if I did that . . .

Dad had been taken to the police station. In my youthful mind that meant he was in prison. The thought of my dad locked up in a cell because of me was too much for me to bear.

As far as I was concerned, there was no decision to make. I was retracting, and as quickly as I possibly could.

'No, Mum, it didn't, it didn't happen,' I desperately tried to assure her.

The relief in my mum's voice instantly made me feel better. She told me that I would have to tell the police and that she would arrange for someone to come and see me right away. I handed the phone back to Nan and returned to the living room to await my fate.

Whether it was that evening or the next day is still unclear to me, but I was being kept at Nan's and hadn't been allowed home. Just as Mum had said, a police-woman arrived at Nan's to speak to me. I knew I had to maintain that nothing had ever happened between Dad and me. It was the only way that I could make things right again. She sat next to me on the sofa and asked me various questions about why I had suddenly changed my story.

Everyone kept asking me why – why had I said such a thing? I realised that I needed a motive, some reason for pointing the finger at my father, but I couldn't think what to say. I knew I couldn't say anything about either of my parents or the lifestyle we had at home as I didn't want any more police involvement or to make Mum and Dad cross again. I said that I was jealous of Andrew, something that I had heard Mum saying on the phone to Nan on various occasions as an excuse for my sometimes 'wild behaviour'. She would often comment that I was 'attention-seeking' and so it seemed the obvious excuse to give.

Nothing could be further from the truth. I adored Andrew. I could never be jealous of him. He was still like my own baby. But this explanation seemed to satisfy both my family and the police, so I stuck to it rigidly, desperate for it all just to go away. I felt guilty for causing so much upheaval in the family, and that I had caused the family to break apart. Paul was at home with

Mum, helping to look after Andrew and Katie. Dad was still in custody, and all I wanted was for him to come home so that Mum would stop being so upset.

The next day, a car was sent to Nan's house to collect Mum and me. I had been told to stay at my nan's until further notice, which was fine by me as there was so much upset going on. Mum had arrived, which was more than a little awkward. I hardly knew even how to look at her, yet I knew how important it was to maintain the lie I had told to keep the family peace. She said that we had to go and see a doctor in Carmarthen, and although I couldn't work out what was wrong with me that needed examining, I thought nothing more of it. With the 'stomach migraines', doctors and tests had become a secondary part of my life by now.

When we arrived, I played with the toys in the waiting area. Two women also arrived and began to talk to me as I waited for the doctor to call me through. One was another social worker. The other was Jayne, the policewoman I had seen the day before at my nan's house.

As my name was called, both Jayne and the social worker asked me who I would like to go in with me while I was being examined. I felt put on the spot as the doctor was waiting, and both these women were looking at me for a decision.

I tried to say I didn't mind, but they insisted. Either

one of them could go in there with me; I had to choose which one. I eventually chose Jayne as I remembered her from my nan's house and I thought she was very pretty. Once we had got inside the doctor's room I realised I had made the wrong decision as Jayne appeared to sit coldly in a chair without even looking at me, whilst the social worker had seemed so nice.

The female doctor asked me to lie on the bed. I had assumed – oddly – that she would want to look inside my ears or make me say 'Ahh' as she shined a torch down my throat. She didn't. Instead she asked me to remove my knickers.

I was petrified. Why on earth did they want to see down there? The horror must have shown on my face and she quickly assured me that I could keep a blanket over me at all times, and that this was a perfectly normal procedure that all ladies had to go through when they grew up. She looked to the policewoman for reassurance and said, 'Isn't that right? We both have lots of these, don't we?' Jayne grunted a response with a brief nod of her head.

I lay back with tears in my eyes, while the doctor examined me down below. More shame. I couldn't believe that this was a 'normal' procedure that all women go through.

When the doctor was finished, I got my clothes back

on and the policewoman took me back to the waiting room. Mum was called in to speak to the doctor. I will never know what was said in there, but Mum returned very upset and tearful.

As an adult I can now rationalise that the doctor was looking for any signs of forced entry. But they would not have been able to find any, as Dad had stopped when he couldn't gain access for intercourse. With my retraction in place, and no medical evidence against him, Dad came home later that day.

The moment my dad came home is something I will remember all my life. I was at my nan's. Indeed, the whole family was there: Mum, Nan, Paul, Andrew and even Katie. I sat on the sofa, staring at the floor, unable to watch him enter the house. Instead of being angry with him for denying the charges, I was scared. I was terrified that he would hate me, and that he would never forgive me for what I had done.

Eventually, curiosity got the better of me. As he walked through the door, I looked up at his face.

In a weary and tired voice, he looked back at me and said, 'All right, Julia . . .'

From that moment onwards, life returned to 'normal'. As promised, the situation was not mentioned again at home. Mum and Dad gave me no reason to believe they hated me or held me responsible for what had happened. Instead they made it quite clear that they believed Mandy and Jan were responsible, and banned me from having any contact with Fliss in school. They even contacted the headmaster and made sure that the school separated us in the classroom. We could no longer sit together.

This was the hardest part for me to deal with. Not only was I living with the man who had sexually abused me for the past two years, living with a family who thought I was a liar and a troublemaker, but I had also lost one of my best friends. Fliss also believed I had made the whole story up. She was furious with me and as the story circulated around the school, typically people took Felicity's side. I was branded a liar. I lost a lot of friends, but couldn't tell the truth. I realised that I had to carry this secret with me all my life. I now knew all too well what the consequences would be if I ever told anyone else and it wasn't worth it. No one would ever believe me again anyway, and I couldn't put myself through the torment of being called a liar once more. Felicity and I had a lot of built-up anger towards one another. She hated me for lying, and I hated her for not seeing the truth.

The animosity between us was intense – so intense we fought one day in the playground. As we kicked, scratched and pulled at one another's hair, all I remember hearing around me were the chants, 'Go, Fliss! Go, Fliss!' The shame of not hearing my name being called destroyed any self-esteem I had left.

I didn't even feel the pain of her nails or the sting of her hand across my face. Right then, nothing hurt any more. I was totally numb.

I thought I had lost everything in my life that meant anything to me. I didn't see much point in carrying on. The lies I had to tell to maintain my story were weighing me down. Mum and Dad arranged for me to see various people – psychologists and counsellors – and each time I would have to repeat the story that I was jealous of Andrew, that I was seeking attention. I was beginning to believe I must be mad. I was telling so many people that I was a liar that I was beginning to think maybe I was.

The only thing that should have come of it all was an end to the abuse. Now that Dad knew my silence was broken, that I had spoken out once, there was no way that he would ever touch me again, surely. He had spent a night or two locked up; he had been given a taster of what his life would be like if he got caught. So I knew that he would never lay a finger on me again. Maybe in time, I thought, I could try to rebuild my life and my relationships with my friends and family.

But Dad was yet to prove me wrong.

7
Here We Go Again

After my retraction, life carried on just as it always had. And that included my father's abuse. The scare of my speaking out didn't put him off. He never discussed the allegations with me; he never made any reference to events whatsoever. He merely picked up where he had left off.

My humiliation was complete. My father's refusal to see that I was crying out for help was a terrible shock to me. I felt utterly worthless and insignificant. That he continued the abuse was the ultimate betrayal and I began to see him in a totally different light. He had had the opportunity to stop, to try and make things right with me, be my daddy again. But instead of battling his perversions for my emotional and psychological well-being, he felt compelled to continue his secret fantasy. At the expense, it seemed, of his own daughter. The realisation of how little I meant to him was the final humiliation.

Maybe he believed that now everyone thought I was a liar, he was safer than before. If I ever said anything again, no one would believe me now. That's what I thought, and perhaps it gave him a sense of security.

I sank into a depression. I was trapped in my situation. I had taken a chance when I had told Fliss my secret, and now I had blown it. I was furious with myself for not having had the strength to see it through. But I was so young, I didn't have the capacity to cope with such a burden.

Fliss and I developed a volatile, love–hate relationship. One minute we would be best friends again, and the next we hated one another with a passion. That, it seemed, was the pattern of my life in general at this time: up one moment, down the next. As soon as I thought I was starting to get somewhere I would be thrown back to square one. My relationship with my mother had begun to improve during her pregnancy, but since my allegations against my father it had deteriorated once more. The closeness we had begun to experience was now eradicated beyond repair. School became the only place where I could try to maintain some kind of stability, and I yearned to be popular and well thought of.

Unfortunately this came at a cost. I would do anything to try to impress my peers, from stealing bags of crisps from the school tuck shop, to sticking up my fingers in defiance at the new supply teacher. I got caught, but the pats on my back from my friends made up for the fact that I got the biggest telling-off of my school history. I smiled inside that at least I had made a good impression with my friends.

I became the class joker, always looking for a new way to win friends and make a favourable impression on the other pupils. This was how my behaviour came to be perceived as 'odd' or 'strange'. My mother even began to believe I suffered from attention deficit disorder, as I acted such a clown at all times. I was so desperate to feel accepted that I began striving for that acceptance in any way I could.

Meanwhile, Dad continued his abuse of me. He couldn't be seen to be making an effort not to be alone with me after the accusations I had made, but he was clever. Situations always seemed to present themselves where he would have the opportunity to make his move.

One day I was sitting in the back of the car after a trip to the supermarket. Andrew had gone up to Nan's with Paul, and Mum was 'cleaning the shopping'. I was sitting behind Dad, out of his reach, I thought, when he put his hand out behind him and began to caress my knee. I just sat there and once again tried to shut off mentally. I knew what was coming, and knew that I was powerless to prevent it.

Dad asked me to sit forwards in order to give him better access. I did as I was told. I held on to the seat in front of me as Dad's hand moved up my skirt. He rubbed his fingers around the edge of my knickers, as usual, before venturing inside. I shut my eyes tightly, waiting for it to end. Usually he would play around a little, rubbing his fingers all over me, but this time he tried to take things a stage further.

I suddenly felt a sharp, piercing pain as Dad tried to push his finger inside me. I gasped and grabbed his hand, trying to push him away. Dad had never hurt me before. He was usually really gentle, whether to prevent me from stopping him from continuing or because he genuinely cared for me, I don't know.

Dad resisted my objections and continued trying to push his finger deeper inside me. I began pushing with both hands against his, desperately trying to stop him. I couldn't believe the pain. It was absolute agony, as though someone had poured boiling-hot water between my legs. He continued to overpower my resistance for a while, keeping his hand firmly in place. Eventually he withdrew his fingers without saying a word. Apart from that first gasp of pain, I hadn't made a sound. I had simply held my breath for as long as I possibly could. I had never felt strong enough to resist him before, but the pain I was experiencing had taken over. My hand pushing his away was almost involuntary.

I sat behind him, squeezing my legs together, in my vain hope that the pressure would take the pain away. Tears stung my eyes, but I refused to allow them out. Maybe this was my punishment for all the trouble I had caused. Even if that was not his intention, it was what I told myself.

From this point on, I decided that I deserved punishment. And, in some strange way, I felt better once I had accepted that I was worthless. Suddenly everything around me didn't seem to matter so much any more. Mum's rules and regulations were what I deserved. If Dad 'messed with me' it was what I deserved. And if friends hated me, hey – what else should I expect?

After I turned eleven, I was to start secondary school. Paul had already enrolled at Cardigan Secondary, the local comprehensive. It was the school most of my friends were going to, including Felicity, so it was decided that I would go to the other school further away. Vicky, my other friend from school, was also going there, so I really didn't mind and even encouraged Mum and Dad to send me. It was both the easy option and a bid to lay the past to rest.

I began this new stage in my life with optimism. I was growing up now, and was allowed extra privileges. I was able to catch a bus with friends and go to town, visit the local cinema and go swimming, and so my outlook on life began to change.

I made lots of new friends, people who didn't know my past, had no preconceived ideas about me, and I found that I was popular and enjoyed my new life.

One girl that I made particular friends with was called Sarah. She was a lovely girl and we became quite close. We giggled together over everything, and seemed to have a lot in common – maybe a little too much.

One day, as Sarah and I were talking, she told me that a family member had been sexually abusing her. My heart sank. All the old feelings and insecurities began to overwhelm me and I found myself telling her that I understood because the same thing was happening to me.

We cried together, consoled one another, and made a pact to talk to a teacher about it. Somehow, knowing someone else was experiencing the same thing made it less scary for me. I began to think that I could actually go through with this. I could make it really stop this time. I had Sarah on my side.

We went to see our head of year, a man called Mr Davies, who was so lovely and gentle that we both felt at ease with him. He spoke to us individually in a vacant classroom, with Sarah going in first. I had no idea what she said to him, but she came out in tears saying she couldn't go through with it, and that nothing had happened after all. I knew what she was going through, I understood that denial, and felt determined that she wouldn't make the same mistake that I had the previous year. Sarah, however, had other ideas, and was adamant that she didn't want to speak to me. She ran off in tears and I was left with Mr Davies calling me in . . .

I panicked. Suddenly I was alone again. I didn't know what to do. The old fear erupted inside me and I felt incredibly scared and unsure that I could actually do this either. Mr Davies tried his best to calm me down, and chatted to me informally about what was going on. I held my panic to the best of my ability and told him the truth. I was unable to go into any detail, but I confirmed that, yes, Dad was sexually abusing me.

Mr Davies then said that he would have to tell the headmaster, and began to walk to the door. Something snapped inside me and what happened next I can only describe as a complete and utter breakdown.

I lunged towards him in a desperate attempt to stop him from telling anyone. I was hysterical, screaming, shouting. I didn't care any more that I was in school and that people could hear me. As far as I was concerned there was no one around apart from Mr Davies, me – and the headmaster who I was so desperate to avoid.

Mr Davies literally had to make a run for the headmaster's office. I ran after him, screaming. I reached the headmaster's door just as he shut it firmly behind him. I began banging on the door with my fists, screaming at him to stop, pleading with him, begging him to do as I asked. I was sobbing hysterically. A group of people crowded around me to witness the commotion. I was completely oblivious to them. All I cared about was stopping this man from ruining my life once again.

I can't remember what happened next. Either I passed out, or I have blanked it out. All I remember is my parents solemnly walking towards me, silently packing me into the back of the car and driving me home.

It was decided that I should leave that school and enrol at Cardigan Secondary with Paul. No further action came of my disclosures. To this day I still have no idea what was said to the school authorities to explain my conduct.

I was back to square one, trapped. My hopes of my life improving had been shattered. I felt as though my world had been turned upside down again. I was angry and bitter that I hadn't seen it coming. I should have realised that no good would come of me speaking out. I had tried before, to no avail. I had let myself down yet again, and ruined any chance of happiness that I may have had. Though the abuse continued, I could shut off from it to a certain extent. My school life and my life with my friends was all I lived for. During those hours I could try to live a normal life, try to be me. Now at Cardigan, I would be the new girl once more. All respite was gone. Everyone else would already have had the opportunity to make new friends. I would be the odd one out. I believed I had failed before I had even begun.

8
Teenage Rebellion

By the time I turned thirteen, the frustration and turmoil inside me were jostling for space alongside new-found adolescent hormones. Most girls at that age find the transition from child to teenager difficult, and that's without the added burden and shame that my parents were subjecting me to.

I didn't know how to cope. There were times when I wanted to scream, let it all out. But I couldn't. Everything had to appear normal to the outside world. I was too scared of someone noticing something was wrong and questioning me. My previous experiences of speaking out had left me fearful of anyone finding out again. My parents branded me as a liar and a troublemaker, and I was desperate for these notions of me not to extend into my outside life, where the abuse had never existed. I had no release for my anger and pain. I carried it all inside. I felt as though I was going to explode. I wanted it all to end.

One day at my nan's I was feeling particularly upset. Alone in the kitchen, fighting back the tears, I grabbed my arm in sheer frustration and dug my nails into it as hard as I possibly could. The pain was strangely relaxing, as though all my anger and tension were being diffused. As my nails entered deeper, cutting into the skin, I began to breathe a little easier. As I loosened my grip I felt that I had completely let off steam, and as I looked down I could see blood on my arm and four identical wounds where my nails had been.

I cleaned my arm up, stopped the bleeding, and then pulled down my sleeve. It was my secret, and I felt almost content. It was something that neither Mum nor Dad could control . . .

That's when I decided I needed another way of relieving my anger. A boy at school had recently had his appendix removed, and had spent a couple of days in hospital. If only that were me, I thought: safe, and away from it all. Somewhere I could just forget. No sooner had the thought occurred to me than I was putting my plan into action.

Clutching my stomach and complaining of agonising pain, I walked into the kitchen to see Mum and Dad. After a while they began to be concerned and called the emergency doctor. Before I knew it, still writhing in agony, Dad was driving me to the local hospital. Keeping up the pretence of such agonising pain was a difficult act to maintain, but the longing to escape my imprisoned home-life was all the motivation I needed to ensure my cries were believed.

That night I had my appendix removed. I remember a doctor saying to me after surgery, 'I know you must be in pain from the operation, but I bet that feels a whole lot better now that it's been removed, doesn't it?'

If only he knew, I thought to myself. Despite the now very real pain, he was strangely right. I did feel better. I was away from home, away from Mum and Dad. I had a few days' peace. I was happy.

All things come to an end, however, and eventually the time came to return home, which I dreaded with all my heart. But because I was ill, once more Mum came into her own, fussing over me. It ensured Dad had to keep his distance. Until I was back on my feet again, fully recovered, he had no opportunity to abuse me.

That year I decided to put matters into my own hands. Enough was enough, and I couldn't take any more. I was a teenager, and with my new-found ability to speak my mind I began to refuse my father's advances. I finally gathered the courage to start saying, 'No.'

If Dad tried to touch me, I would move away. If he asked me to touch him, I would refuse. After five years of co-operation, Dad found my refusals hard to take. Although he never tried to threaten me to continue, or forced me physically, he started to use other tactics to try to encourage me to co-operate with him sexually. He began offering me money: £2 if I let him touch my breasts; £20 if I let him have sex with me. Every offer he made, I stuck to my guns and refused. It was always hard to refuse as I had become so accustomed to being subservient. However, as time went on, it became easier to resist, and I gained courage with each success.

Instead, I made damn sure that I would always have an excuse for refusing his money and started to make my own. I began washing cars, and then progressed to working in grocery shops, restaurants, hotels – anything at all that would give me enough work to save up my own money. I would work all the hours I could, regardless of the law. I worked weeknights after school, weekends, holidays – any hours that were available I took with open arms, so keen was I to break free from the life that had tormented me for so long. I was eager to create a new life for myself, one that included as little time at home as possible.

Mum and Dad took the majority of my earnings away from me. They insisted that I needed to save for my education, and that I would thank them one day when I was at university. I really didn't mind, as long as

I had enough money to go shopping occasionally with my friends, or to go to the cinema.

It would be natural to think that now the sexual abuse had ended I was happy and ready to move on with my life. In reality, the complete opposite was true. I found it even harder to fit in with the rest of the world. Mum's way of living remained the same and was causing me even more problems now that I was entering adolescence. I yearned to have the freedom my friends had, to be able to choose my own clothes and discover my own identity. Mum's restrictions made this impossible. And I was still living with the man who had abused me sexually since the age of eight. I was battling with the fact that I still loved him as my father, but at the same time I hated him for what he had put me through. I harboured huge resentments towards both my parents.

I needed to release some tension and began to discover ways of hurting myself, without having to hide any scars and without the need to be hospitalised. I began making myself sick. After I had eaten I would find the nearest toilet, push my fingers to the back of my throat and bring up the contents of my stomach. Many people believe bulimia to be about weight loss and dissatisfaction with your physical appearance. For me, it was something inside that I was trying to expel –

a feeling, a notion of myself. I hated myself for what had happened to me, and believed I needed to punish myself. If I was punished, I would feel better.

Friends at school began to notice the pattern of eating then going to the loo, and followed me to see what I was up to. My secret discovered, they threatened to report me to the teachers if I carried on. I tried my best to alter the pattern that was fast becoming a habit and, after a time, their watchful eyes and perseverance paid off.

With no physical outlet for my anger, my emotions didn't take long to reach boiling point once more. I no longer knew where to turn, or what to do next. I felt I had exhausted every avenue. I turned inward, feeling the same depression I had experienced before hanging over me like a cloud.

The school noticed my deterioration and the deputy headmistress took me aside one day after class. She asked me what was wrong, if there was anything I wanted to talk about. The hard exterior I had tried so hard to cultivate began to crack. She was usually such a forbidding teacher, and her sympathy broke my resolve. I didn't know how to cope with her kindness.

I couldn't tell her about my dad. I had tried that before, and the horror of what had happened in my last school still haunted me two years later. Instead, I decided to confide in her about the way my mother made us live. This was, after all, the lesser of the secrets I had to carry, and a revelation I assumed wouldn't have any consequences. I could tell from her dumbfounded reaction that what had become my normality was very strange indeed to the deputy head. She asked if I was aware that these rules and regulations were not right, and that Paul and I were being exposed to unusually unfair restrictions.

I cried as she asked me if I would be willing to write down for her each of the rules and regulations by which we lived. I agreed to do it, and made a list of everything I could think of.

- Not being able to touch anything in the house
- Not being able to choose my own clothes
- Having to run naked to the shower in Mum's room
- Mum having to bring me a towel after a shower
- Not being allowed friends over
- Not being able to get a drink or something to eat
- Not being allowed to sit on the furniture
- Not being allowed home until eleven o'clock at night
- Having to have my hands, face and feet washed

on entering the house
- Not being allowed to touch my school bag until it was cleaned
- Having to ask to use the toilet
- Not able to touch my drawers and wardrobes in my room
- Not able to have a bath . . .

I was sure there were loads more, but just scribbled down the ones that I could remember from the top of my head.

Armed with this, the deputy head said she would see what she could do.

Towards the end of the day, I was summoned to the headmaster's office. I panicked for a moment, wondering what I had done wrong. As the headmaster called me in, I could see two women behind him in the room. I began to experience the same feelings as when I had arrived at the Social Services' offices with Mandy, Jan and Fliss when I was ten. Fear welled up inside me.

The head introduced the two women as social workers. My heart sank. They explained that I had made some disclosures about my life at home that had given them some reason for concern. They asked me about my mother's behaviour and I confirmed the information I had disclosed earlier that day. The social workers explained that they needed to speak to my parents about it, and that it wasn't appropriate for me to go home while things were being discussed.

They asked me if I knew a girl called Alia, who was in my form at school – I did. Alia was in care, and lived with a foster family in Cilgerran. They explained that if I was happy to do so, I could go home with her that night until things were sorted out. They said that someone would come by to see me later that evening, but that for now I should catch the bus home with Alia.

I began to feel relieved. Even though I still held my dad's secret close to my chest, someone was at least acknowledging that what I had been going through at home was not normal. I didn't want to go home anyway, so the thought of going home with Alia was a welcome alternative.

I couldn't wait to go to a house with some normality. For a moment I didn't even care that Mum would be cross with me for speaking out, or what the consequences might be. I was just pleased to have been given some form of escape, and this time it was an escape that, though far from permanent, didn't involve any pain.

After school finished, I sat on the bus with Alia as though I was just going to a friend's house to play. I put to the back of my mind the fact that Social Services were going to talk to my parents and busied myself with thoughts of what we might have for tea, and what Alia's room would be like.

Her foster parents greeted me and introduced themselves as Lyn and Dave Bantten. Lyn and Dave had three boys of their own – Scott, Luke and Darren – and two foster daughters – Alia and Deanna. Deanna was in the year below me at my school.

Lyn and Dave made me feel very welcome and Alia and I soon forgot the formality of the arrangement and contented ourselves with playing upstairs. Alia and Deanna shared a room. The mere fact that they could do as they liked in their room amazed me. I loved the freedom and wished I could stay there for ever and live their life. Mine, in comparison, was bleak. I had barely glimpsed what a life with few restrictions was like, and was bitter at my exclusion from this 'normality'.

Before long I was visited by the social worker who had come to school earlier that day.

Mum and Dad had been informed, and I was petrified to learn what their reaction had been. But as I entered the living room, I was greeted with kind and sympathetic smiles – an encouraging welcome that nevertheless did nothing to relieve the nausea washing over me.

The social worker explained that she had been to see my parents, and had discussed with them the regime at home. Apparently my parents completely understood how I felt, and my mother had promised to get some help with her compulsive behaviour. The social worker explained that having been assured that my parents would co-operate, she couldn't see any reason why I couldn't return home that evening. If I wanted to get my things together, she would take me.

Hearing this, the sickness in my stomach should have eased. Surely this was the answer to my problems? I was refusing Dad's advances, Mum was going to get help, things would change . . . So why did I feel complete and utter panic at the prospect of going home? The past five years had taken their toll on me physically, emotionally and psychologically. Now that I had made my escape, I didn't want to go back.

Maybe Mum and Dad were pretending to understand. Maybe they would be cross with me when the social worker had gone home? What if Dad wouldn't take no for an answer any more? Maybe this would be my punishment for speaking to the authorities again? I couldn't bear to go back to the desperate way I had lived all those years. I stated quite firmly that I was not going home.

Eyebrows were raised. My social worker wanted to

know why I didn't want to go. Was there anything else I hadn't told them? I considered telling the whole truth and exposing the lie I had lived since Dad was first investigated. But the fear of not being believed was too great for me to risk it. I had a chance to be happy, to be safe, and I didn't want them to think I was making it up, as people had thought before. Despite the support I had received when I had spoken out previously, Mum had made it quite obvious that she had never believed me. Since retracting my allegations both when I was ten, and in secondary school, I had a reputation for 'storytelling'. I was convinced that no one would ever believe me if I tried to tell the truth now. As the fable goes, there are only so many times you can cry 'wolf' before people stop listening.

I shook my head forcefully. I think they could tell that I was holding back, but no one pushed me. I was told that if I didn't want to go home then I didn't have to, that I could stay with Alia that night if I wished.

Back upstairs with the girls, I felt a mixture of emotions: relief that I hadn't been forced to return home, but also anxiety, knowing that this arrangement couldn't last. I churned over and over in my head whether or not to mention my dad to them. Maybe these people would actually believe me and I wouldn't have to live a lie any longer? Alia and Deanna asked me why I didn't want to go home. I paused. I looked at their faces – and broke my resolve. I told them everything.

These two girls knew social workers better than anyone. They had spent their lives in foster care. If anyone was in a position to advise me, it was them.

Their reaction was incredible. The support they gave me was immense. Once again I broke down under their kindness. In many ways it had been easier to cope with not being believed than with acceptance and under-standing. I crumpled as I poured out how I had been living a lie, that what I had told the police three years ago was true, and how I had never 'made it up', as so many people now believed.

Alia looked me in the eye and said, 'You have to tell Lyn, and if you don't – I will.'

I felt the usual hysteria begin to build up inside me, but this time I fought against it. I knew she was right. How could I go home and live this life any more? I needed to be free of the deceit that had dominated my life. I agreed that Alia could tell Lyn.

I sat on the spare bed in the girls' room and shook. I knew that Alia was downstairs talking to Lyn and I was convinced that the grown-ups wouldn't believe me. Surely they would just think I was 'attention-seeking', as I had heard my mother say constantly on the phone to my nan, as her reason for my allegations. My mother herself was convinced or trying to convince herself that I had been jealous of Andrew, and so believed I had used such 'stories' as a means of getting attention. Deanna tried her best to reassure me and keep me talking, but I found it difficult to follow the thread of conversation.

Soon enough, Alia returned, informing me that Lyn wanted to see me in the front room.

Each step I took was a burden. I had to physically force myself to descend the staircase. As I entered the front room, I glanced at Lyn with fearful anticipation. She returned an empathetic look of reassurance.

Over the next hour I told Lyn everything I could remember: what had happened and why I hadn't told anyone.

After I had finished my story, she said, 'You do realise that I have a duty to call the social worker and tell them what you've just told me, don't you?'

I nodded. I was older this time round. I wasn't so naïve. I now knew that speaking out had consequences and I knew only too well what those consequences would be. But this time I was far enough away from my parents not to have to witness the turmoil my revelations would cause. I hoped that that was enough to keep me strong.

Once again, all hell broke loose. A social worker came to the house. I was asked lots of questions. But everyone was on my side. People believed me and were showing me support. I began to think that I could start to be 'me' again. I didn't have to live a lie any more. I could at last shake off the burden that I had carried around for so long.

The next day I was interviewed by two women – one was the original social worker allocated to me and the other a policewoman I had never met – and my disclosures were videotaped. I was taken to a building, the exact nature or location of which I have no recollection, but the room was bright and airy. The women sat in two chairs, and I was directed to a sofa. A couple of dolls lay on the table in front of me, but these did nothing to distract my attention from the video camera in the corner. The women began their interview by talking to me about 'truth' and 'lies'. They asked me to think of examples of each in order to determine that I knew the difference. I gave simple childlike responses, feeling extremely insecure. I began to worry about whether these women thought I was the liar I had been portrayed as for the past three years. As the interview progressed, they asked me to say exactly what had happened between Dad and me. I couldn't find the words to explain, and felt helpless even to try. The fear of not being believed overwhelmed me.

To save me the embarrassment of explaining in words they suggested that I use the dolls to show them what had happened. I was grateful for this diversion, although the shame as I pointed to the dolls' 'privates' somehow felt even worse than using words. I cringed as they repeated back to me what I was showing them in order to clarify that they understood, and nodded fiercely. I wanted the words they had uttered to disappear.

When the interview was over, I returned to the Banttens' house and was told I would be staying there for the foreseeable future. I knew that Dad was being investigated, but I didn't want to know any more. The details would have made me even more unhappy, and I preferred to try to carry on with as little information as possible.

Life at the Banttens' that summer soon became routine. However, after some time it became necessary for me to move to another foster home. My placements were short term as plans for my long-term future had not yet been made. I moved in with the Clarkes in Llandysul.

Alana and Stuart Clarke were slightly older than Lyn and Dave and were lovely, caring people. Theirs was a quiet household, unlike the busy atmosphere of the Banttens', with only one other foster child named

Leanne. Leanne was only seven years old, and so I was the only teenager in the house. I had my own room and, to a certain extent, could do as I wished. Finally I had the perfect, normal existence I had always dreamed of.

But, despite this new standard of living, the experience of living in care with no roots had left me feeling extremely depressed again. This time, however, my depression didn't involve the old feelings of frustration and tension. This time I no longer cared what happened to me. I had given up.

My new life consisted of various court appearances. My guardian *ad litem*, Sally, who had been appointed to me by the courts, would collect me from the Clarkes' house and take me to court. I never really understood what the court appearances were for, and never learned what was decided in them. All I knew was that people kept talking about care plans and court orders for my protection. Afterwards, Sally would collect me and take me back to the Clarkes', where my life would carry on as before.

I became very introverted, and began to wish I had never said anything at all about Dad. I felt lost and it seemed to me that life at home was at least familiar. I didn't feel as though I fitted in anywhere. I didn't know what my place in life was and really started to pine for some normality and security. Normality was the one thing I had been searching for my whole life. It was the one thing I had always pined for. Slowly, the realisation dawned on me that, however distorted it might appear to others, for me 'normality' meant home with Mum and Dad. I didn't know how to cope with anything else, and so I began asking the Clarkes if I could go home.

My introversion was noticed by my social worker and I was encouraged to make contact with my mother. When we spoke on the phone, no reference was ever made to the investigations surrounding Dad, which had been going on for five months now. It was all just general chitchat and small talk, an attempt to give me back some of the 'normality' I was missing. I had supervised contact with my mum with a social worker present, and over a couple of months I resumed some regular contact with her.

But my closest relationship at this time was with my social worker, Buddug Ward. It was Buddug who told me that it had been decided I was to return home. It was now December and apparently Dad was still being investigated, but the fact that I had rebuilt a relationship with my mother and had been asking to go home for some time meant that Social Services thought it safe for me to return home on condition that my mother didn't leave me alone with my father under any circumstances. Buddug would continue to be my social worker, and would meet me regularly to check I was OK, and to give me a chance to talk to her about how things were going.

I was surprised that I was being allowed to return home to live under the same roof as my father. However, after my experience of life in foster care, I was just pleased to be returning to familiarity. I didn't complain. As far as I was concerned, I would have the best of both worlds. Back to life as I knew it, but without Dad's abuse, and with Buddug to talk to and support me whenever I needed her. I couldn't see a better solution to the problem.

The day I left Alana's for the last time, I hugged her with an awkward embrace. I had grown afraid of physical contact with people, preferring to avoid it unless absolutely necessary. But Alana had been good to me and had given me the space I needed to come to terms with my time in foster care without any expectations of me. For this, I was grateful.

That day in school seemed to be the longest ever. I looked at my watch countless times to see how long it would be before I made the bus journey back to my home.

I saw my brother Paul in school that day. We

acknowledged one another like mere acquaintances. After my five months in care, it was as though we didn't really know each other any more, and I knew that he held me responsible for the upset our family had gone through. No one in my family believed the accusations I had made against my father.

Little did I know at this point how damaging it would be to lose my support network and return to a household in which I was branded a liar.

After the school bus dropped me off at my stop, I made the walk up Lady Road to the estate in Glanarberth. I could see Morgeney at the bottom of the hill, and walked towards the door, feeling like a stranger. Mum opened the door at my arrival, told me to take off my shoes, and enter the house.

The weeks that followed remain a blur. If I thought I had been depressed during my time in care, then I was mistaken. The way I felt now that I was back at home was ten times worse. Yes, initially there was a 'honeymoon' period, where Mum and Dad would tiptoe around me being as nice as possible, but that wore off soon enough and they quickly reverted to their opinion of me as a liar. Dad would simply agree with anything my mum said, and would look at me as though I was mentally unstable. The way they treated me made me start to think that maybe they were right. Maybe it was all just in my head. How could I prove otherwise?

My only support at this time was Buddug. She could see that my confidence and determination were ebbing away, and kept asking me again and again what was happening at home. I longed to be able to tell her, to talk about how I was being made to feel so small, but I just couldn't find the words. Her constant reassurance that what I had been through was not my fault was starting to fall on deaf ears. All the good work she had done with me began to fall apart.

Mum came into my room one night, about two weeks after I had arrived back, and gave me a present. This in itself was an odd gesture. But the gift I unwrapped had even more meaning. It was a fridge magnet – ironic, really, seeing that we weren't even allowed in the utility room, let alone physically to touch the fridge. The magnet was in the shape of a bear doing aerobics with, emblazoned on its big belly, 'Would this body lie?'

Mum left me alone to digest my gift, but I knew exactly what she meant by it. This was her way of telling me that I was lying, and that I had to retract once more. The emblazoned words were the message Mum was trying to get through to me. I clutched the magnet and began sobbing hysterically on my bedroom floor.

Mum immediately walked back into the room and sat on my bed. She looked at my tears, and coldly asked, 'Do you have anything you want to tell me?'

I knew this was my cue. I knew what I was supposed to do. How could I go against her? While I was in care, I had kept my resolve to tell the truth for five whole months. I had stuck religiously to what I knew in my heart to have happened with Dad. But now, living with people who didn't believe me, and having to face Dad every day knowing that I had told his secret, had worn me down. Five months of building my strength and determination had been quashed in two weeks. I told Mum what she wanted to hear.

Mum's face was a picture. She was elated. She rushed out of the room, eager to call the authorities and stop the investigations surrounding my father. Everything from thereon was a whirlwind of activity once more. The next day Mum and Dad remained on the phone calling various people. Everyone seemed busy and preoccupied. I stayed in my room, feeling as though life wasn't worth living. When Buddug arrived later that day for our session together, she quizzed me about the retraction. I gave bleak, monotone answers, knowing that she could see straight through me. But despite Buddug's attempts to understand why I had retracted, I knew that I had to keep up the façade. By this point, I was tired of talking about me and my life. I needed to retreat inside myself and pretend none of this was happening. I'd had enough.

Dad was concerned that Buddug would eventually get through to me, and so began proceedings to get my social worker changed. He sat me down in the kitchen one day soon after my retraction and told me to write a letter stating that I didn't want to see Buddug any more. I did as he said and, sure enough, Buddug was removed from my case.

The new social worker, Paula, knew only that I was a child who had made and retracted allegations of sexual abuse on two separate occasions. We never bonded or developed a relationship as I had done with Buddug. Mum and Dad seemed content with this and were happy to keep Paula as my social worker. I missed Buddug with a passion.

And this was how life went on. The investigations into my father were once again discontinued. We carried on at home without mentioning my five months in foster care, and my relationship with my family continued in a strained fashion. Eventually, Paula stopped visiting. There were no further disclosures being made so Social Services saw no further need to maintain access.

From this point on, I stopped thinking about my past with Dad. My coping mechanism now was to continue with my life and pretend nothing had ever happened. I had to convince myself it hadn't in order to survive. One day I would be able to leave home for good, but, until that time, I decided that I should live my life to the best of my ability. I resigned myself to a life of denial and learned how to face the dubious looks of contempt with a new hardness that showed I didn't care. And by this point, I really didn't.

9
Growing Up

Between 1995 and 1997, from the age of fourteen to sixteen, I went through a period of teenage rebellion. Every opportunity I had to be away from home, I grasped with both hands. And if Mum or Dad wouldn't let me attend the latest party, or go to another sleepover, I would run away from home. Every weekend I had a full diary, and regularly stayed with friends, whose parents didn't impose the same restrictions as mine. We pretty much did as we pleased.

I worked as many hours as I possibly could. While I had been in care I had had to give up my part-time job in the local grocery shop as the social workers had realised that the hours I was working were illegal. But now that I was back home and no longer under the supervision of Social Services, I found various waitressing jobs.

It was during this time working in a local coffee shop that I met Stacey, a girl from my year in school who also worked as a waitress there. Despite being in the same year we had never spoken before. We soon became very close and spent as much time together as possible. I was surprised how much we had in common. At weekends, after work, I would stay at Stacey's house. Her mum had died years earlier and she lived with just her dad; my mum thought that it was nice for us to be spending time together. As far as my parents were concerned, Stacey and I stayed home and watched videos. But at the tender age of fourteen or so, gone were our days of pizza and Coke in front of the TV. We wanted to live like the adults we thought we were, and saw ourselves as much older than our years. I'm sure if my parents had known the real reason for my sleepovers, they would not have encouraged our time together.

A typical weekend at Stacey's house would involve us going back to her place after a waitressing shift. Music would blare out loudly as we applied thick make-up with the precision of artists at work. Then we would choose what to wear, discarding item after item in a crumpled heap on the floor until we found perfect outfits for the evening ahead.

Then we would hit the town. We always started in the same pub, aiming to get drunk as fast as humanly possible, before moving on to the next, and ending up in the local nightclub at the end of the evening. Before setting off, we would often down a two-litre bottle of strong cider from the off-licence to give ourselves a head start on drinking and save some of the cost of drinking in pubs. We would also buy our ciggies for the evening, and would think nothing of chain-smoking a pack of twenty each throughout the night, buying more if necessary.

Enjoying these nights out was a secondary concern. On my part certainly my primary intention was to get as drunk as possible. All I cared about was boys, and would regularly compete to see who could 'pull' the most men in an evening.

And that was how I lost my virginity. David was no-body special. I was at a house party – drunk as ever – and he was simply there. We ended up wandering off alone, and walked up a little hill a few hundred yards from the house.

There, in a drunken haze, we somehow managed to fumble around on the ground, undoing what little of our clothes needed loosening to enable us to have sex. It was over in minutes. And as I lay there with stones and gravel digging into my flesh, I wondered what on earth all the fuss was about.

I had changed from the depressive, introverted girl I had been for some years into someone who, on the surface, was sexually confident. But I was seeking a comfort that I believed only men could give me. The message that my father had laid down in my fragile mind was that people who loved you acted sexually towards you. Sexuality meant that people cared, that they loved me. And I craved this attention more than anything else. It would take some time for me to realise that sex without feelings was pointless. At that moment with David, I thought that it would never be possible for me to enjoy a sexual experience with a man. There and then I resigned myself to a future of simply complying with anyone who wanted sex with me. I desensitised myself to such an extent that it simply didn't occur to me that I had a choice about whom I slept with. But I knew that my sexuality could work for me as a tool to gain the acceptance and admiration of which I had grown so needy.

For the next couple of years I was quite promiscuous. I had no self-worth whatsoever and would have sex with anyone who wanted me. I had no boundaries or standards, and felt as though it didn't matter if men used me. Mum's obsessive behaviour was much the same as ever at home, and I knew there was no way I could hide something like the pill from her. She still took my school bag from me when I got home, carefully examining and wiping down each item in the kitchen, before replacing them in the bag, carefully ensuring no mess was made. The day I went to the family planning clinic I called her on my way back to school, and informed her that I had been prescribed the pill for heavy periods. Over the phone, I wouldn't have to witness her reaction.

She seemed a little hesitant and surprised that the clinic hadn't offered an alternative but I managed to satisfy her with my explanation.

During my wild nights out with Stacey, I began experimenting with drugs – nothing more than cannabis, but it soon became a regular thing at the end of an evening that Stacey and I would drop into a dealer's flat to get stoned. We would chill out at the end of our night partying, before stumbling back to her house to fall into a drunken stupor until morning.

The hardest part would be going home the next day, still nursing a raging hangover, but trying my best to act as together as possible so that my parents wouldn't suspect a thing. I would often have to work a shift at the coffee shop, running to the toilet every ten minutes to be sick.

At fifteen, I took a job at the hotel where Paul worked as a waiter. We soon became quite a team and we developed a new-found respect and liking for each other. For a couple of years, Paul and I worked as many hours as possible in between school and studying. A bond developed between us that we had never experienced before, and I valued it immensely.

But Paul could also see how damaging my behaviour was becoming. I was a complete flirt, and soon had all the guys at the hotel running around me. Paul could see I was on dangerous ground and often commented how frustrating it was that I would 'come on' to all his friends.

I didn't know how else to act. My idea of men had been completely distorted. I didn't know how to be with a man – any man – without acting sexually. I had no concept of what normal behaviour is like between a man and a woman. At the time I behaved in the way I had been taught. I used sex as my tool.

Flirtation came easily, and I found that I could generally use it to my advantage. This manipulation mirrored how my father had manipulated me over the years. Using his sexual advances to secure my silence had won him his goal, and in return for my co-operation over the years, he had instilled in me the notion that sex was all men wanted. It took some time for me to realise that men could also be trusted. But before learning this, I would make many more mistakes.

Life at home had improved little. We were now allowed to sit on the sofas as long as the throws Mum put on them remained in place, and this felt like a privilege. It was certainly a step up from sitting on the floor. But Mum still expected us not to touch our wardrobes and drawers, and although we no longer had to strip naked in the kitchen when we had a shower, we were still expected to leave our clothes in a pile in our rooms and run naked through the hallway, to the en suite in my parents' bedroom. Being sixteen years old and fully developed, this was a procedure that obviously caused a lot of upset and embarrassment. Despite Mum making sure that Paul was in his room, and that no one was looking, I hated having to run through the house, bare and exposed.

We still had our hands and faces washed down with baby wipes, and we still wouldn't dare to make a drink or something to eat in the kitchen. If I wanted to do my hair and make-up before going to school, I had a designated space in the hallway in front of the mirror. If I dared to brush my hair in my bedroom there would be hell to pay for the stray hairs that contaminated my room.

By the time I was sixteen, Mum and Dad knew that I was going to pubs and clubs. One Christmas Eve I told them I was going to a staff party at the coffee shop and asked for a lift into town. There was no such party organised, but some of the staff were meeting up in town and going out for a few drinks. One of the older waitresses, Sharon, had arranged to meet me, and we would make our way to the pub together.

As Dad drove me into town, supposedly to the staff party, I suddenly shouted, 'Hey! There's Sharon! Can you drop me off here, please? I will walk up with her.' Thankfully he did, and I thought I had succeeded in my devious plan. Little did I know that he had driven around town passing the coffee shop to make sure the party was on as I had described, and knew full well I had in fact gone to the pub, as he suspected. After the initial telling-off when I got home that night, my parents seemed to resign themselves to the fact that I was a wayward teenager, the 'black sheep of the family' and so we arrived at a compromise. I could go out with their consent as long as I was picked up at a designated time and place. I think they realised that I would have gone regardless, and so met me halfway.

It was 1997 and I had done extremely well in my GCSEs. Despite the constant partying and self-destruction I had obtained three As, six Bs, one C and one D, which had completely baffled my mother. Indeed, everyone in the family had expected me to do badly, and their lack of faith had rubbed off on me. Even I had to look twice when I collected my results, and I realised for the first time that I wasn't as daft as I had been led to believe. I had a bright future ahead of me. I could achieve anything I wanted to achieve. I felt excited at the prospect of joining the sixth form, getting through my A levels and going to university.

In the sixth form, most of the girls had steady boy-friends. I was still experimenting with guys, but hadn't felt secure or safe enough to let anyone in particular get close to me. However, on a sixth-form trip to Ireland I got to know a boy called Dorian, who was in the year above me at school. Everyone, even the teachers, was in holiday mode. Throughout the first evening Dorian and I got on better and better, and by the end of the evening we returned to my room together – a room I was sharing with three other girls.

Dorian and I cuddled up together in my bottom bunk, and fell asleep in each other's arms, blissfully unaware of the others around us. It was strange for me to have an experience with a guy that didn't involve sex. Previously it wouldn't have mattered to me whether there were other people present or not if the guy wanted to take things further, I always felt helpless to object. Saying no was something I was unaccustomed to, nor did I have the confidence any more to say it.

The next morning, we were awoken by the door being barged open, and Dr Morgan, my head of year, appeared in the doorway. He had obviously been searching for Dorian since his absence from his room the night before, and wasn't best pleased.

Dorian and I looked guiltily at one another. It was obvious what people thought had been happening between us. This whole experience was new to me. I didn't know how to behave towards him. I wondered what would come of this new relationship. I was very unsure of myself and whether I could handle the commitment of being with one person and allowing him to get close to me.

But back at home I began to spend the majority of my time with Dorian. At weekends he would pick me up in his car to take me out for the day, or we would go back to his place to listen to music. Mum and Dad would always invite him in, which was unusual as we had never been allowed to have friends over. I had made Dorian aware of my past, as I was very conscious that he might hear something from one of his friends. I didn't want him to pass any judgements. Dorian certainly never seemed to let it affect his relationship with my parents. Quite the opposite, in fact. He would spend his time chatting in the kitchen with my parents, keen to make a good impression, rather than spend his time with me. I found it very difficult to understand, considering the years of abuse he knew they had subjected me to.

One school lunch-time we found ourselves alone at a holiday cottage his parents owned. I had grown quite used to the idea of us not having sex, and felt quite scared at the prospect of taking things further. It was easier to have sex with complete strangers with no emotional connection, as I had done several times since David. I never had to see them again. But this felt personal. I wasn't sure if I was ready.

But it was typical of me that, not wanting to offend or upset him, I nodded in agreement to his request to have sex. He took me into the bedroom, and began kissing me. I found it hard to kiss him back. My stomach began the old, familiar churning. Despite my string of one-night stands, this intimacy scared me rigid and I felt powerless to do anything about that fear. I simply couldn't say no.

Slowly, Dorian began taking off my clothes as I clung to him in sudden insecurity and embarrassment. I didn't want him to see my body. I didn't want him to look at me. I felt dirty and ashamed for the first time since my father's abuse. He kept asking me if I was OK, if it was OK to carry on. As he lay me down, I was grateful to be able to look past his shoulder and away from his gaze. And as he moved up and down against me, tears streaked my cheeks. What was wrong with me? I just didn't seem able to function in a relationship. Surely this wasn't what sex with a partner was supposed to be like?

As soon as it was over, we scurried around fishing for our clothes in an attempt to hide our embarrassment. It was awkward and tense, and we drove back to school in silence, separating without as much as a kiss. We made a clumsy goodbye, promising to meet up soon and practically ran away from one another. I think Dorian felt awkward because I was so obviously not comfortable with the situation. I was pretty sure it had been his first time, and despite how deeply he felt for me his embarrassment was quite apparent. Despite Dorian's sincere and genuine nature, I still felt dirty and ashamed, as if I had been violated. I knew that he cared about me and that if I had said a direct 'no' he would have stopped. But I just didn't have it in me to argue. My father had conditioned me to think that a man's needs were a priority in a relationship. I didn't feel as though I mattered.

My relationship with Dorian went from bad to worse. He began to care a great deal for me, and began telling me he loved me. I wasn't even sure if I was capable of love.

One evening, we were walking through town when Dorian asked if I would go with him to meet his friend Johnny. I felt extremely disgruntled that our 'date' included seeing his friends, especially a friend that I didn't even know, but typically I bit my tongue and walked along with him.

As we approached Johnny, I could see his bright blue eyes sparkling beneath his dark deep-set eyebrows, and thought he was the most amazing guy I had ever seen. His gaze transfixed me.

My heart melted. Even his voice seemed to turn me to jelly. The whole experience taught me one thing: I certainly wasn't supposed to be with Dorian. I didn't experience that magical feeling with him as I did when I met Johnny.

A couple of weeks later, with our relationship increasingly strained, Dorian and I bumped into Johnny at a fair.

Not one for rides, Dorian turned to Johnny and said, 'Hey, Johnny, you'll take Julia on the rides for me, won't you?'

Johnny turned to me. 'Come on,' he said. The twinkle in his eye told me that he wasn't only being polite.

We sat close together on the big wheel, pinned down by a safety bar. As the ride began, I nervously giggled, partly from fear and partly from the pure excitement of being alone with him. As the cage picked up speed and began spinning, I screamed along with everyone else, and Johnny leaned over and put his hand on my knee in reassurance. It seemed an eternity before the ride came to an end, and he removed his hand for the bars to be released. I looked up into his eyes to gauge his response, and he smiled back at me intensely. I was sure he felt the same way.

I made my decision to end the relationship with Dorian. A couple of days later, my opportunity came as Dorian started telling me how much he loved me. Once more, I couldn't bring myself to say it back.

He said, 'You just don't love me back, do you?'

'No,' I replied, 'I'm sorry, but I don't.'

The time I would have spent with Dorian I spent with Stacey. We began going swimming every week after school with another friend, Sapphire. She asked Dorian and Johnny if they also wanted to come. Not surprisingly, Dorian didn't. But Johnny decided that he would . . .

As we laughed and chatted together in the pool, the chemistry between us was as strong as ever. I could see Stacey and Sapphire smiling and encouraging me as if to say, 'Go, girl!' I could feel his body against mine, which sent shivers down my spine. He gazed adoringly into my eyes, and asked if I would like to go out with him sometime. As I got out of the pool and sauntered into the ladies' changing rooms, I felt as though I was the sexiest, most desirable woman in the world.

Nothing could have dampened my spirit at that moment. The excitement and elation were like nothing I had ever experienced before, and I never wanted it to end. I now knew what people meant by 'love at first sight'. That's exactly what it was – love.

Jon, as I called him, was also aware of my past but, unlike others, he refused to accept it. One night, a few months into our relationship, I had run away from home, met up with Jon at a party and spent the night at a mutual friend's house. We stayed up all night talking. I told Jon all about my past, and cried in his arms as I practically relived every moment of the years of abuse I had been subjected to. Jon just held me tight, silent tears flowing down his cheeks as he listened.

Telling Jon felt safe. I knew he trusted me, loved me, and never wanted to see anyone hurt me ever again. He wanted no contact whatsoever with my parents, and grew angry at the mere mention of them. He refused to come to my house, and point-blank ignored them if they were ever in his presence. This made life very difficult but I had utmost respect for his determination to protect and stand by me. Jon couldn't bear to think about what I had been through. Given half the chance he would have quite happily taken my dad on himself – something I fought hard to keep him from doing.

After a year with Jon, the strain of living at home became unbearable. Jon had shown me how good life could be, and I wanted nothing more than to be with him 24/7. The restrictions my mother imposed at home still stood, and now, aged seventeen, I realised that my life didn't need to be this way. Jon and I decided to set up home together.

Jon was eighteen and studying at college in Cardigan, and despite me still being at school, studying for A levels, we were adamant that we could make things work between us. Jon's mum, Jean, decided to respect our wishes. Despite her obvious concern about the direction her son's life was taking, she saw something between us that was special. Jon had made her aware of my abusive history, which compounded her resolve to make sure we were both OK and safe. Jon and I simply adored one another and would have done anything to be together. Jean supported us all the way and helped us to find our first flat.

My parents, however, did not feel the same way. While Jon disliked them, they hated him with a passion. I think my father saw him as a threat, and wanted the relationship to end before Jon could have the opportunity to convince me to do something about our past, fearful of what the consequences might be if I finally found the courage to speak out once and for all.

We had some fabulous times in our first flat. At the weekends, Jon and I would go out together, dancing the night away with no time restriction on when to go home, and we thoroughly enjoyed every moment of it. I continued working in the hotel to earn some money, and Jon began working part time for his stepdad, Paul, so that we could afford to eat and pay our rent.

I don't really know what made me yearn for a child at seventeen years of age. I think I just wanted to be able to love someone and give them the upbringing that I wished I had had. I began craving a baby, and would drop hints into conversations about what a perfect little family we would be, and what good parents we would make.

Jon loved kids and seemed quite happy to dream along with me about how 'one day' we would do just that. And when my contraception became erratic he just smiled and said, 'Well, if it happens it happens!'

Sure enough – it happened.

I did a test alone at home one day after school, before Jon came home from work.

I picked up the test . . . and turned it slowly over . . . and looking back at me were two pink lines. I was pregnant.

I had wanted there to be two lines there, had

desperately wanted the result to be positive, but now that it was I didn't know what to do.

My initial reaction was to see Stacey. I needed to talk to her, needed to hear from someone else that everything was going to be OK. I ran up to the café where she worked but it was so busy I couldn't get near her. The run up the road had cleared my head, and I began to calm down a little and get used to the idea that there was a little person growing inside me.

On my way back to the flat, I saw a worried Jon walking towards me. He had been home to the flat, found the empty pregnancy test box on the floor, and was wondering what on earth was going on. He looked at me and asked, 'Are you pregnant?' The last thing I wanted to do was have this conversation in the middle of the street, so I begged him to come home and I would explain everything there.

Once back inside, his big eyes searched my face. Suddenly I was unsure of what his reaction would be. 'Yes,' I replied. 'Yes, I am pregnant.' A smile spread across his face from ear to ear as he flung his arms around me in absolute joy. His reaction gave me permission to feel excited myself. We lay all night, holding each other tightly, stroking my non-existent bump.

We were desperate to tell our families, Jon's mum

first. We were nervous about how she might react. I was still only seventeen and we had been together only a year. We braced ourselves for what might be a very negative experience. As we stood in her kitchen the next day, Jean knew instantly that something was wrong. But when I looked her straight in the eye and said, 'I'm pregnant,' she was overjoyed, thrilled at the prospect of becoming a grandmother. Even Jon's younger brother, Matthew, came to give me a hug. I felt so at peace with the support I had around me, and really began looking to the future. It seemed strange how only recently my life had seemed so bleak, and now I had so much to look forward to. My former life seemed a distant bad dream.

I knew that telling my parents would be a much harder task. They had never warmed to Jon, and would be horrified at the prospect of a child cementing us together for the rest of our lives. We decided to tell them on neutral ground in case things turned nasty. I called my mother and asked if she and Dad could meet us for a coffee and a chat.

Jon and I sat at a table in the coffee shop, waiting. Mum and Dad arrived with Nan. I was disappointed. I would have liked to have told my nan separately. On her own she probably would have understood but it was possible that after witnessing my parents' reaction, she would be as disappointed with me as they were sure to be.

It was obvious from their faces that they knew something bad was coming. They strode across to our table with stern expressions, asking straight away, 'What is it?' We hadn't even had a chance to order any coffees.

I murmured, 'Erm . . . well . . . I'm pregnant . . .' the last word drifting off as my mother burst into tears and walked out. Nan stayed seated next to my dad, bewildered as to what to do for the best.

Dad looked at me. 'So,' he said, 'when are you getting rid of it?'

I couldn't believe what I'd heard. It just confirmed to me that he really couldn't care less about me. Surely any normal father, even if he didn't want a teenage pregnancy for his daughter, would at least ask what she wanted to do. I had expected Mum and Dad to encourage me to have an abortion, but this response summed up my dad's controlling nature. As far as he was concerned, the baby had to go and that was that. I, however, had other plans.

But back at home, my parents' negative response, combined with a mixture of morning sickness and hormonal imbalance, left me feeling very down. Jon tried his hardest to keep my spirits high and to support me, but I was seventeen, pregnant and missing my mum. To a certain degree, I never really had my mum anyway. But I just wanted her to understand, and to love and support me through this, and I knew that for as long as I was with Jon that would never happen. Whenever I had been ill at home, Mum had been fantastic. Now that I was feeling so incredibly sick all the time, I craved that motherly attention, and remembered how close we had become when she was pregnant with Andrew. I yearned for that closeness once more.

By Christmas I had tried to rebuild my relationship with my mum, and was beginning to make progress. She had given up trying to persuade me to have an abortion and we had begun talking on the phone again. I would tell her how sick and unwell I felt, and how, with the strain of mock A levels coming up, I was finding it hard to cope. All I wanted to do was go home to Mum. I felt so low and unwell that I reverted back to the child I suppose I still was. I just wanted someone grown up to look after me, and I knew that despite how hard poor Jon tried he couldn't give me what I needed at this time.

I asked Mum if I could go home. She refused. She said that Dad didn't want me to go home, that I had made my bed and I should lie in it. I'd never felt so rejected. Once more, Mum was sacrificing me for her husband and it broke my heart that she wouldn't have me home and make things better. I pleaded with her, begged her to have me back. I don't know what came over me. I just couldn't cope. I wanted all the responsibility I carried on my shoulders to disappear.

Eventually, Mum talked Dad round. She called me one day to say that I could go home, but that it had to be when it suited them and that she would let me know. Poor Jon had to live in our flat with me, knowing that I was leaving him, and he had to live with that until my parents decided that it was 'convenient' for me to go home.

The day before Christmas Eve, of all days, Mum called to say I could go home. I packed my bags and left. Jon and I said our goodbyes, and put a reluctant end to our relationship there and then. What a fool I was – the one man in my life who had only ever tried to help and support me, love me unconditionally, and I walked away from him as though he didn't matter.

Back at home, I spent my days being sick. My mock A levels were in the January, during which I would occasionally have to run out of the classroom and leave the exam, only just making it outside before throwing up all over the floor. Teachers would ask me with sympathetic smiles if I suffered from nerves. But when I told them I was pregnant I was met with looks of disdain.

The entire pregnancy continued with some difficulty. The stress I was under meant that I ended up dropping out of the majority of my A levels, managing in the end to sit only my English exams. I was nine months pregnant, with the school on standby in case the stress sent me into labour.

Jon, I heard, had gone to America for six weeks. He must have been tormented since we split, knowing that I was back home with my parents, carrying his child. At my twenty-week scan I had discovered that I was carrying a baby girl – an additional concern for Jon, knowing that I was back living with a paedophile.

I was in absolute denial. I couldn't begin to think of what had happened between Dad and me. I felt weak and ill the majority of the time, and couldn't bear to add any additional worries to my already fragile state. Any concerns regarding Dad went to the back of my mind and I was determined that's where they would stay.

10

And Then There Were Three . . .

Home had initially felt like a haven, somewhere I could forget about the responsibilities ahead, and give myself a chance to come to terms with the prospect of becoming a mother. Home was my 'normality' and, despite how unhappy I had been there over the years, it was still the place that made me feel, in my way, whole, secure.

Mum had always been good to us whenever we were ill as kids, and now that I was pregnant she was content to fuss over me, directing antenatal appointments and buying the things I would need. I think my pregnancy gave her a motherly purpose she hadn't really had before. It was as if, for the first time, she could now contribute effectively towards me as her daughter, and I lapped up the care and attention. Mum and I grew closer and, as I began to look forward to the new arrival, sometimes I thought that maybe we had turned a corner as a family.

But then there was Dad.

Despite my efforts to forget the abuse he had subjected me to as a child, I couldn't have a normal relationship with him. I didn't know how to behave in front of him. I wanted things to be right, as though nothing had ever happened, but that was impossible when I didn't even know how to look him in the eye. Every time he passed me, my body would tense. I felt uncomfortable in his presence, and he made it quite clear that my return home was not his decision. Every time he looked at my growing belly, I felt ashamed. Although I adored my growing figure in private, in front of my dad it felt like a sexual statement, and it evoked the old feelings of guilt and shame, which made me feel dirty.

We tolerated each other's presence, if only for my mother's sake, but there was no great love or emotion between us. I mourned the loss of my father as though he had died. The daddy I remembered from my life in Essex was a distant memory. The man I once knew had left me when I was eight years old, and I didn't even recognise the impostor who had taken his place. I looked at him as though he were a stranger. To the outside world nothing had changed, and I was the only one who saw his transformation. Not being able to voice these feelings left me immensely frustrated.

*

Living back at home meant that I could spend more time with my younger brother, Andrew. I had always been close to him, almost as though he were a son of mine. Over the years he had been through a lot himself, and was eventually diagnosed with the autistic spectrum disorder, Asperger's syndrome, as well as dyspraxia. Once he had a diagnosis his behaviour made more sense. He had suffered from a lot of developmental delays as a child, and as a result had always seemed 'different' from his peers.

Andrew, ten years younger than me, was only eight. He had to abide by the same rules and regulations that Paul and I had lived by although he never seemed to complain. I wondered if his learning disabilities made the regimes at home more acceptable. His incomprehension of social norms may have delayed his realisation of the dysfunction in our family.

With Jon away in the States I felt even more alone. The confidant and soul mate I had trusted with my life had gone. I had pushed away the one person who accepted me for who I was. Unconditional love was something I was not accustomed to, and I had now lost my opportunity to have a future with the only man who had made me feel like me. After years of being groomed emotionally and sexually, I didn't know how to be myself. The real Julia had been lost somewhere along the way, and I had no idea how to find her.

Jon was coming home for the birth of our baby. I hoped that maybe the birth would bring us back together, that we could re-ignite our relationship.

When he arrived back, he called me and we arranged to meet in a local coffee shop to catch up before the birth. Mum and Dad were dubious about my meeting Jonathan as they were determined that we should be kept apart but I really didn't care what they thought. I had to see him.

When we had split, I couldn't bear to think what it might mean. Finality hadn't entered my head. I had known only that I needed to go home to come to terms with the pregnancy and feel that security that being with your parents brings – however distorted that view of 'security' was in my head. At the time I had simply to switch off my emotions towards Jon in order to cope, something that I had become quite accustomed to doing over the years. Now, almost seven months later, I knew that somehow I had to make things up to him. I had been only two months pregnant when I had moved back home; I was now almost nine months pregnant and had to hope that he still loved me, despite everything I had put him through. Would I even still feel the way I once had about him when he was sitting in front of me?

When he arrived, he scanned the room, fixed his eyes on me, and strode across to sit at my table. His smile was so endearing I struggled to reason how I could ever have left him.

I suddenly became aware that I was huge, nine months pregnant and probably about as appealing as a hippopotamus. I cringed with embarrassment. I desperately wished I was a slender, sexier version of myself. How else could I capture his heart as he had just done mine? As he sat down, he commented on how well I looked. I blushed – feeling suddenly like the teenager I still was.

We talked for ages – about America, the baby, anything and everything except the real reason I wanted to see him. I wanted him back. I suggested we go for a walk along the bay, to which he nodded in agreement. We wandered through town, then down by the riverside, and stopped to sit on a bench overlooking the bay. I summoned up all the courage I had, and told him how I felt – that I still loved him; how he was everything I had ever wanted. Jon looked at me with hurt in his eyes. I could see how much pain I had put him through, and it was obvious that he was afraid I would do that to him again.

I cried, held him tight, and I begged him to trust me, to give us a chance. This was the man I wanted to spend the rest of my life with.

After some time, he turned to me. He told me that he loved me, and we kissed as though for the first time.

As I returned home, I knew I had to tell my parents that we were back together, and knew that they would be far from pleased. Somehow, though, it didn't matter. My baby was on the way, and I was back with Jon. I realised that I had everything I had ever wanted.

As I walked through the door, my elation at being back with Jon must have beamed from my face. My heart felt lighter than it had in months.

My parents hit the roof, told me how the whole thing would be a disaster, how he wasn't welcome in their house. But their words flew over my head. I didn't care what they thought any more. Jon and my baby girl inside of me were all that mattered.

I continued to live at home, and Jon lived with his mum and stepdad, Paul. Nine months pregnant, I would travel there on the bus as often as I could. A week before my due date I had a false alarm. My due date came and went. Six days later, the pains started once more.

In the hospital, grinding my teeth, I pushed with all my might for what felt like hours. And then Molly-Jayne was born. All the pain of labour melted away as soon as she arrived. The instant love I felt for her was beyond anything I could have anticipated. For that moment, as I held her in my arms, I felt whole again. I had a purpose. I examined every little crease on her skin. Each tiny finger and toe was so delicate, so perfect, that I could hardly imagine she had been curled up inside of me these past nine months.

As I looked at her face, I felt so proud of our little family. The fact we were still kids ourselves seemed irrelevant. The urge to protect this tiny child overwhelmed me. Here was my chance to make a difference, to give a child the life I had always wanted for myself. I had an opportunity to make things right, to compensate for my own childhood and nurture this baby like the little girl inside of me who never had the chance to grow up herself.

But the next day, one of the doctors who came to examine her took one look at me and said, 'Oh, God, please don't tell me you're the mother?' I felt ashamed, as though I didn't have the right to be called her 'mother'. I had such low self-esteem and poor self-image that his judgement took away all the happiness I was feeling. I didn't for a second entertain standing up for myself. I was completely conditioned to being sub-servient. I just nodded in reply, to which he asked: 'And how old are you? Fourteen?' I mumbled that no, I was eighteen, but he didn't appear to be listening. He merely shook his head and continued examining my baby as though I wasn't even there.

My parents came to see me the next day and I couldn't look my father in the eye. My father's presence made the thoughts in my head link this beautiful baby with the act of sex, a connection that always intruded when he was around. I felt uncomfortable and, suddenly, the most natural thing in the world felt wrong. All the old feelings of shame, stress and anxiety came to the surface.

At odds with this ill feeling was the fact that I couldn't wait to get home and settle in with my new baby girl. But Mum said that she wasn't ready for me. She told the nursing staff that I would have to stay in hospital a few days, as that was the earliest that Dad could collect me and take me home. I was devastated. All I wanted to do was take my baby home and get to know her without the watchful, judgemental glances of the ward staff. But I knew it was pointless arguing with Mum. It took me back to when she had left me in the car with Dad because she wasn't 'ready' for me to go indoors after doing the shopping. It was then that my life had been turned upside down. Years later – even though I was an adult – she was still dictating my life.

When the time came it felt strange to be going home with Mum and Dad now that Jon and I were back together. I hated the thought of us not being with Molly as a family, sharing the parental responsibilities. I asked him to visit the following day whilst my parents were out.

The following day Jon duly arrived and we spent the time cuddling Molly and making plans. The time flew by and I jumped when I heard my parents returning.

I knew that they wouldn't be happy that Jon was in their house, but I hoped that they wouldn't want to cause a scene, and that I could hold off the inevitable ructions until Jon had gone.

As Mum opened the door to my room, I held my breath, awaiting her reaction. 'MIKE!' she screamed, calling my father. 'He's here, he's in the house!' My father appeared, livid that Jon had the 'audacity' to enter his home.

Jon kept saying, 'Molly's my daughter!' I defended his right to be there too, but nothing either of us said seemed to make the slightest difference. My father asked him to leave. I bade him a teary farewell. I knew that he wouldn't be able to see us at the house again, and I promised that I would make the journey by bus to meet him at his parents' house the next day.

As I closed the door behind him, I turned to face my parents. I no longer felt dread or fear. I was angry. We argued. My mother eventually stated, 'If you don't like it you know where the door is. Pack your bags and leave.'

I'd been plummeted from ecstasy into hell. I couldn't take this way of living any more. I decided to do just that. I went to my room, packed as many things as I could for Molly and me and went to bed without saying a word. The next morning, I got up, dressed Molly and announced to my parents that I was leaving. They didn't bat an eyelid.

I had been out of hospital for two days. I was a teenager with a six-day-old baby in my arms, and as many belongings as I could possibly carry. I must have looked a sight as I stood at that bus stop, but from the moment the door shut behind me, I decided I had left my parents' home for good.

We got the support we needed from Jon's mother, Jean. It was only a matter of days before she found us the most perfect little cottage to rent. It was such a quaint little place, Jon and I fell in love with it immediately. We moved in within the week, and busied ourselves decorating the nursery with big bright drawings of Winnie-the-Pooh.

I was still very fragile inside and was unable to cope with stress or anxiety. My strategy was to block out most of my thoughts and try to concentrate on feelings and instinct. Jon was not aware of this battle within me. I tried to carry on to the best of my ability without my parents in my life, and put all my efforts into my relationships with Jon and Molly.

We began to make plans for our future. We were determined that, despite having a child so young, we would still make something of ourselves. Jon applied for a college course in Llanelli. This would mean a lot of travelling back and forth every day on the bus, so we decided to move to Llanelli to make things easier. Having made this big decision, that night, as we lay in bed, we talked until the early hours about what our new life would be like. The move to Llanelli would mean that we were alone, away from our families, and would have to stand on our own feet. We began to get excited about the adventure of living in a new town, as we fell asleep to the sound of Molly's gentle breathing at our side.

We eventually decided on a small, terraced, two-bedroom property, with a pretty little enclosed garden behind it. We loved it, and the location seemed ideal, only yards from a huge lake with dozens of swans and ducks. I could picture us taking Molly there to feed them at weekends.

After some time, my parents made contact with me. My mother telephoned occasionally, which soon progressed to them coming to visit us. My thinking about my family was confused. I missed having them around me, and felt complete when I had some contact with them again. Living that much further away struck a perfect balance. I didn't have to see them every day, but they were there if and when it suited us all. I felt the arrangement worked well, but Jon was not entirely happy with the interaction. He and my parents learned how to tolerate each other, but there was never any love lost between them.

In general, Jon and I were happy, and for a while that was all that mattered. But the finance Jon had been awarded for his studies was fast running out and, with no other income to rely on, our financial position deteriorated. By Christmas 1999, we were completely broke and couldn't afford to eat. Oddly, this had no real impact on me as I continued my strategy of blocking out anything that brought on stress and anxiety. We arranged with Jean that we would stay with her for three weeks – the week leading up to Christmas and the two weeks after – and we soon settled in to enjoy the relaxed atmosphere of her home.

Each evening, we would sit up late talking with Jean and Paul, Jon's stepfather. Jon had told them of my past soon after we first got together; Jean had said that if I wanted to talk about it, she was there. But when talking about the abuse to people previously, I had always done so in a very matter-of-fact manner, almost as though I had been talking about someone else. Jon was the only person to whom I had ever really shown my true feelings. I found it difficult expressing such difficult and painful emotions at the best of times and couldn't imagine talking to Jean about something that I couldn't really admit to myself. To a large extent, I was still in denial about the abuse, and refused to accept that, despite what had happened, my parents were capable of this behaviour. The sense of family loyalty I still maintained was almost cultish. Jean suggested that I might want to write a journal about the things that happened and that I could give it to her so that I wouldn't actually have to say the words.

I felt more comfortable with this suggestion, and I sat down that night with a notebook and pen and tried to put into words everything that had happened with my dad. Surprisingly, I found it really easy to write. It was almost therapeutic to put into words what he had done to me, and I wrote ferociously for hours until the account was complete. It was almost as though I had taken the plug out of the bath: however hard you try to stop the water from pouring out, it just keeps on running.

Once I'd got it all down, I felt a sense of satisfaction

and was eager to give the journal to Jean. I thought it would help me start to face my past and deal with the things that had happened. I hoped that Jean might be able to help me through that journey. I had had no formal counselling and had only survived by blocking out my past and refusing to face it. I knew that wasn't healthy. Once Jean had read my journal, perhaps I could start letting go of some of the pain I was carrying. If somebody else knew everything about my story and they still cared about me, surely that meant that I wasn't to blame?

New Year's Eve morning, I was dozing in bed as Jon played with Molly. She was sitting on his lap as he held her hands, gently lifting her up and down from sitting to standing as she squealed with laughter. Molly's squeals suddenly changed to a high-pitched scream. I leapt out of bed, desperate to discover what had caused her distress. She was lying on Jon's lap with her arm bent awkwardly against her chest.

I screamed at Jon, 'What have you done? What have you done to my baby?'

He looked as distressed as I was, and explained that he had been playing with her, lifting her up and down, but then she hadn't moved with him . . . He had pulled on her without her co-operation and it looked like he had broken or sprained one of her arms. Furious, and scared, I scooped Molly off his lap and ran into the kitchen. Molly was in agony and I wanted to get her to hospital as quickly as I could.

I told Jean what had happened. She was furious too, and screamed for Paul to take us straight to the hospital.

Thankfully, Molly's arm wasn't broken. Her elbow had dislocated, which the doctor said was common in children. He could see how upset and distressed we both were and reassured us that it could happen to anyone.

Despite this, I found it very hard to forgive Jon for hurting our little girl. Jon was beside himself and felt terribly guilty, but still I focused all my pent-up stress and anxiety on him. I knew that it had been unintentional and that now Molly's elbow was back in place she was no longer in pain, and I tried to forgive Jon for the accident. But I was seething. We decided to go home to Llanelli early. I was eager to have Molly to myself again, almost as though I could make things better by having her close to me back in our own home.

A couple of days later, there was a knock at the door. Jon had a key and we didn't know anyone else in town. If my parents were coming over they would have called. I walked towards the door hesitantly, almost whispering, 'Who is it?'

The reply that came was a bigger surprise: 'It's Social Services.'

My heart skipped a beat. Why on earth were social workers coming to my house? I had had no contact with Social Services since my time in care, and I had no intentions of having them back in my life now. My view of social workers was negative. As far as I was concerned the system had done nothing to help me when I was a child, and had sent me back home to live with my mother and father. I had tried to move on with my life and had become reconciled with my parents, but I still didn't view Social Services as an organisation that had done me any favours over the years. I opened the door, and demanded of the two people standing there what they wanted.

'Can we come in please?' was all they would commit to at the door.

Reluctantly, I held it open for them and watched them suspiciously as they entered. I followed them into the living room and sat down. I repeated once more: 'What do you want?'

I had assumed, due to my past, that their enquiries would involve me. So I was shocked when they responded, 'We're here about your daughter, Molly.'

Someone had obviously reported the accident with her elbow. Maybe the hospital had a policy of following up such injuries, but we honestly had no idea. Obviously, when Social Services had done a check on my surname, it would have alerted them to my past. They asked if it was true that my father had sexually abused me as a child, and wanted to know what sort of contact Molly had with him now. I became very defensive. I admitted that Molly did see my father, but that I had never left her alone with him and that she only ever saw him when both my mother and I were around. I assured them that her safety was paramount. After some time, they left, giving me their number if I decided I wanted to talk to them at any time.

I was furious. I was convinced that I was cursed by my childhood. Every time I had tried to move on, things turned nasty. Yet again, I vowed that I would never mention what had happened to me, that I would bury my secret deep in the back of my mind. Every emotion, every pain I felt, I put into an imaginary box and tightly shut the lid.

II

Wedding Belle

Despite the constant uphill struggles that Jon and I faced, we grew together as a couple, stronger with each day that passed. He turned to me one day, asking so casually if I wanted to get married. I laughed at the blunt way in which he proposed, and accepted. Without a doubt, I knew that Jon and I would be together for ever, and I felt ready to make the commitment. Our finances were strained, so the wedding would have to remain on hold whilst we saved, but as far as I was concerned, what we had together was worth more than money, and getting engaged was enough to make me feel loved and secure.

We re-evaluated our career plans and decided we had no choice but for Jon to leave college and get a job. We desperately needed a regular income and were young enough to study at some point in the future if we decided we wanted to.

We began looking for work, but Llanelli is a small

town and there was nothing for Jon. We were forced to look slightly further afield, to Swansea. Jon was offered a position in the DVLA, which forced yet another move.

During this difficult time, my parents had a huge influence on our lives. My father knew Swansea extremely well and was able to advise us which areas to avoid and which were reasonably priced. Mum and Dad even drove us around, looking at properties to rent.

I was able to separate mentally the different people my parents were. I could put 'Dad the Abuser' in one box, and still see 'Normal Dad' in front of me, and the same with my mother. I separated her into 'Obsessive-Compulsive Mum' and 'Normal Mum'. It was how I was able to continue living life without losing my sanity.

But Jon was confused by my ability to distinguish. He couldn't differentiate between the two. For him, my father was a paedophile. The friction this caused was indescribable. But Jon stuck by me, and with my parents' help we eventually decided on a two-bedroom house in Waun Wen, and moved in that February.

Living so far from anyone we knew, I began to feel quite isolated, so started to look for work for myself. Dad helped me land a job at the bank he worked for. I interviewed well, and was desperate for a chance to show what I was capable of. I looked at various childcare establishments to find something suitable for

Molly. Luckily, there was a nursery just around the corner from our house that I could easily walk to every morning. After viewing and having a chat with the nursery manager, Molly was enrolled. I felt guilty leaving her for the first time, but I knew that financially we would be better off if we were both working. Working families' tax credit went a long way to covering Molly's nursery fees, so the money we earned could be put towards a better standard of living. We were desperate to survive independently, not wanting to have to ask our families for hand-outs. After years of working as a teenager, hard work wasn't something I feared and I relished the opportunity to make something of myself. On 10 April 2000, I started work. I felt strangely nervous walking through the doors. I was nineteen and had never had a 'full-time' job. I had something to prove because my dad already worked for the company. I was keen to make new friends, and be accepted for who I was. I needn't have worried. Working for the bank brought me more than just a job and a salary; it gave me the space I so dearly needed to find myself and experience what it was like to be just 'Julia' rather than a fiancée, a mum, a daughter, a survivor of sexual abuse.

I quickly gained confidence. I felt as though my work was appreciated and that I was making a valid contribution. I took on extra responsibilities and strived to prove myself at every opportunity. In fact, I became almost obsessed with gaining acceptance and praise, and would try to find new tasks and projects to busy myself with. I needed to occupy myself to the extreme. I had to have as many projects as I could manage on the go at once to feel safe. As soon as one project was completed I couldn't rest until I found another to fill my time. The constant motion, the occupation of my headspace with other things, allowed me to hide from the inner turmoil of my personal life.

What began as a healthy lifestyle choice quickly turned into a self-destructive path that would inhibit my true emotions for years to come. This destructive cycle became the centre of my existence. I didn't know how else to survive, and felt fearful of reverting back to the quiet life I had had in Llanelli – where it was just Jon, Molly and me. I wasn't sure if I was capable of keeping my demons locked away if I had the time to confront them and so I didn't give myself the opportunity to find out.

Anyone and everyone around me became an enemy. I would lash out at people if I felt them getting too close to me, fearful that if I let them in they would hurt me, and the pain of being hurt once more would be too much to take. My own family had let me down all my life, yet I loved them regardless. I had grown accustomed to loving people, wanting them near me, yet always waiting for the day that they would betray me. I found it hard to trust anyone.

And that included Jon.

I adored him, loved him with an intensity that scared me. But it was this fear that made me start to push him away. How could I trust him not to let me down? If I was the one pushing him away, then I was the one with control. At least that way I would have made the decision. I could influence how I got hurt without the betrayal coming up and biting me before I had time to see it.

Jon and I began arguing, and they were arguments that I would often initiate to test his commitment to me. I would push and push him further away from me. I was trying to convince myself that I didn't need him, didn't want him in my life. If there was only Molly and me to worry about, then no one could let me down.

By September, I had finished with Jon again, though we remained amicable. I found it difficult to be in a relationship, yet I found it difficult not to be in a relationship. It was a Catch 22. I was addicted to affection – I had come to depend on feeling loved to feel secure inside myself – but I was unable to let anyone get really close to me.

From an early age my father had taught me that

sexual attention is the equivalent of love, and I yearned to fill that need I had grown to depend upon. To experience this with a stranger felt safer than letting in someone I truly loved. It didn't really matter who made me feel special.

Affection was like a drug to me. I needed it to feel whole, couldn't cope without it. As soon as I felt it lacking in my life I would search for my next fix. Though Jon had fulfilled this need in my life, I had found the intimacy too much to handle. Now that I had pushed him away once more, I began a relationship with a customer from the bank – Peter. A friend at work took me to one side and warned me that she knew Peter, and that he spent a lot of time in his local pub. I appreciated her concern but disregarded the warning, confident that I knew what I was doing. I needed to fill my life with as much activity as possible to distract me from the real issues that needed my attention. Starting a new relationship filled that gap of loneliness, which meant I could continue a while longer in oblivion.

Our first date give me a warning sign that things weren't right. Peter got blind drunk, and I practically had to carry him home. I didn't care. He showed me affection and made me feel worthy.

My own negativity attracted negativity. The fact that Peter had problems of his own didn't bother me. I was too engrossed in mine. Jon had been too good for me. I had found it hard to relate to him. He was such a good man with good intentions that at that time I felt as though I had nothing in common with him.

Even so, I tried to re-evaluate my life, and realised that I needed to break the negative pattern. I was in a downward spiral. The stress I was under was beginning to make me feel physically sick, and I wondered whether the stomach migraines I had experienced as a child had returned.

I begged Peter not to drink. I was desperate for him to be sober; desperate for our relationship to work. I spent more and more time over the next three months at his house, and would regularly stay overnight. Molly would always come with me, as I began leaving her travel cot permanently constructed at his place in anticipation of our arrival. Our sexual relationship was very one-sided. He was never interested in using contraception and I was incapable of insisting. Where sex was concerned I was conditioned to be subservient and was incapable of going against his wishes in case I lost his love and affection, which I felt was all that was keeping me going

Soon I knew that Peter drank too much for my liking and that there was no future for us, but I didn't know how to go about changing the cycle. The stress was awful, and the stomach pains continued. To eliminate causes I decided to do a pregnancy test.

I couldn't believe it when the test showed positive. I'd been blocking out the possibility of pregnancy along with everything else. I felt so stupid. How could I not have insisted we use contraception? I should have said something. I had been so irresponsible, and hated myself for getting into such a mess. This wasn't how having a baby was supposed to be. Pregnancy should be a happy occasion, not riddled with guilt and shame. Now that I was in this position I realised that I couldn't stay with Peter. I couldn't have a baby with a man I didn't love. In fact, I didn't even like him any more. I looked at my behaviour, trying to make some sense of my actions. I couldn't have this baby. I couldn't be tied to Peter for the rest of my life. I knew that the only way I could be completely free of him was to have an abortion.

I made an appointment to see my doctor. He was completely dismissive. 'It's people like you who make doing this job as hard as it is.' He refused to sanction me for a termination referral, telling me instead to go home and 'think seriously about your actions'. I returned to my doctor a few days later, adamant that I wanted a termination. He reluctantly put my referral through.

Why did I keep doing this? I was destroying my life

and the lives of everyone around me. I decided I had to start trusting people. That was the only way that my life was going to get better. If I actually let people in, I could start living a normal life. I decided to try to trust Jon. We were still good friends and I needed a friend more than ever at that moment. The next day we met, and I told him everything – about Peter, the baby, everything . . .

Jon once again became my rock. He didn't ever condemn me for my actions or accuse me of acting irresponsibly. He simply listened, offering support and advice when needed. I thought he might disapprove of my plan for an abortion, yet he offered to support me through it. When my appointment came through to go to the hospital for a scan and approval from a second doctor for the termination, it was Jon who went with me. As I lay on that bed whilst they scanned my uterus, I turned away from the radiographer, disgusted with myself. I was sure that she was judging me, and saw me as a foolish teenager who had only herself to blame. From her perspective it was very straightforward. From mine, it was horribly complicated.

I had confided in my mother about the pregnancy and she came through for me once again. She stood by my decision without condemnation and offered to come with me when the time came for the procedure. I had to wait until I was nine weeks pregnant, living for that time with the fact that I was carrying a child that was growing with every day that passed. I tried to push any thoughts of the baby to the back of my mind, the only problem being that that space was rapidly becoming full.

When the date for the abortion came, Mum accompanied me to the hospital. As I sat in my hospital room I was grateful for her being there. She stood by me and my decision with extreme loyalty and I saw a different side to her. Yes, there was no doubt that my childhood had been a torment, that her obsessive nature had pushed me to my limits, but now when I really needed her, she was there for me, and I really respected her for that.

It was time to say goodbye to my baby.

When I awoke from the anaesthetic, I felt strangely still and silent. The emptiness was overwhelming. I knew I had done the right thing, and had no regrets, but I couldn't help but mourn the loss of my child. Mum kept asking me if I was OK. I had to keep reassuring people around me that I was fine. After all, I had got myself into this mess in the first place. I didn't feel I was allowed the privilege of grieving.

As we left the hospital, Mum asked me to stay with her for a couple of days, to get some rest. Back at my house I asked Jon if this was OK with him. Molly was still only eighteen months old and Mum thought that I could do with a couple of days without having to run around after a baby. Jon agreed to take care of her, and Mum took me home with her.

Once I felt stronger I began to miss Molly terribly and was anxious to get home to her. Mum and Dad were reluctant to take me home, and kept trying to persuade me to stay longer. But I was adamant and after a couple of days they gave in and drove me home. I think they were hoping to keep me away from Jonathan for as long as possible. They could see that we were starting to become close again and they would have done anything to keep us apart.

We began spending more and more time together. If Jon wasn't staying with us, then Molly and I were staying at his place, and before long we made the decision to try and make a go of it once more. Jon moved back in, and we joined forces to overcome our problems.

Peter became a part of my past, although I would never forget what I had been through.

I visited a psychic not long after and her words left me chilled.

'Your son's here,' she said.

I looked at her, full of scepticism, thinking she meant Molly. She's guessing, I thought, and did nothing to guide her, thinking instead that I would let her try and 'read' me.

'Not a child in this world, as you have a little girl. I am talking about the child in the spirit world,' she said.

My heart felt as though it stopped beating inside my chest. I stared at her in disbelief.

'He says he's OK, and that you're not to blame. Does this make sense to you?'

I just nodded in agreement as the tears streamed silently down my cheeks.

Now that Jon and I were living together again we felt stronger than ever. Molly was growing up fast and we soon began thinking about having another baby. We had always wanted a big family. I was adamant I wanted at least four kids and thought that a small age gap would be better for Molly. I wanted her to have a brother or sister to play with rather than to baby-sit. I wanted to create a big, loving family to compensate for my own family's dysfunction. I wanted my children to be able to confide in me about anything, to be certain that I was always there for them no matter what. I had always dreamed of a relationship like that with my own mother.

With the abortion still fresh in my memory, I felt as though I had to make things right, and having another child would go a long way towards making amends. I fell pregnant almost immediately, much to our joy, and we revelled at the prospect of becoming parents once more.

Meanwhile, Mum and Dad were going through a difficult stage. Dad lost his job at the bank, supposedly through no fault of his own, and he began appealing against the decision. He told us that he was accused of ill-advising clients for his own financial gain. He stood by his claim that he was acting in the interest of the clients but I was always dubious of his defence, knowing how manipulative he could be. Any appeals he made he lost, and he was left unemployed and with no source of income. Having been very comfortably off, suddenly my parents were in danger of losing their home.

Paul had gone to university in York and Mum dropped the bombshell that she and Dad and Andrew would move up there. It was decided that my nan would also join them and relocate to York. Her health had begun to deteriorate, and she had suffered from a series of mini strokes leaving her quite confused and disorientated at times. My parents couldn't leave her as she now needed daily supervision. They had nothing left in Wales, and a cloud had always hung over them since my allegations as a child. Relocating to York gave them the hope of a new start.

I was devastated. I knew full well that the 'allegations' I had made were all true, despite how hard I was trying not to face it. I was hurt and embarrassed that they were trying to use me as a scapegoat for Dad's malpractice. This was typical of his manipulative and callous attitude, and it frustrated me that I was the only one, apart from Jon, who could see it.

I really wanted my mum around for the baby's birth. I was worried about staying in Wales with no family near me, but I had no choice but to busy myself with my new family instead of moping.

Katelyn Marie arrived at the start of 2002. I now had two beautiful daughters, and felt blessed. Katelyn was a perfect baby; she just slept in my arms so contentedly. The love I felt for her was overwhelming and tears prickled my eyes at the mere sight of her.

Jon and I decided to cement our relationship once and for all, and set a date for the wedding. I was eager to marry as soon as possible. We knew that the time would come when we would have to sit down and discuss who was coming, the seating arrangements, who was giving me away, speeches, etc. But I tried to put it off for as long as I could. I knew how Jon felt about my family, yet I was so desperate for the fairytale wedding I didn't want anything to be amiss. Sadly, because of what they knew about my family, both Jean and Jon's younger brother, Matthew, decided not to come to the wedding. They found it too hard to accept that my father would be a part of the proceedings. We had a close relationship with Jean, and she supported us continuously; this, however, was just one step too far that we were asking her to take.

Eventually, as the wedding date came closer, we had to discuss the issues we had both avoided. I told Jon reluctantly that I wanted my dad to give me away. The pain in Jon's eyes spoke volumes. I knew how he felt, and respected his devotion to me, but all I wanted was a normal life. I didn't want to live the life of a victim of abuse. I wanted more than anything to be normal, and in my mind that could only be achieved by denying my past. By leaving my childhood memories locked in that box, I thought I could continue living under the illusion that I was 'normal' and that my parents were 'normal', when in reality that couldn't have been further from the truth.

Jon knew that this wedding meant the world to me, and was powerless to stop me from proceeding with plans for the day of my dreams. I tried to mention the details as little as possible so as not to antagonise him, but the stress of the situation began to take its toll. Jon organised matching suits for the men in the wedding party. He was heartbroken when I got my father's measurements and ordered him a suit identical to Jon's.

Mum and Dad kept saying that they wouldn't be able to attend the wedding. They said they just couldn't afford it, and we would have to go ahead without them. Jon thought this was fabulous news, but I couldn't bear the thought of getting married without any of my family there with me. I begged and begged them. One minute they would agree and say they were coming; the next Dad would say they couldn't make it after all. But I decided to save up and pay for my parents to attend. That way they couldn't use money as an excuse. I paid for Dad's outfit, paid for their bed and breakfast, and even organised a minibus to collect them on the wedding day and to take them to the church and back with my nan and brothers. They no longer had any excuses, and agreed to attend.

I should have listened to Jon. I should have listened to my parents. But for my perfect day I would have done anything to influence things so that they fitted in with my expectations of what a wedding day should be.

I hardly saw Mum the morning of my wedding. Our relationship was never particularly hands on, so it was

Jon's stepmum, Cath, whom I asked to help me into my wedding dress. Mum was furious that I hadn't asked her. She seemed oblivious to the fact that it would have been uncomfortable doing such an intimate thing together. Despite Mum and I always being close when I was ill, they were the only times that a closeness ever really existed. I had felt comfortable having Mum present when I had been in hospital having a termination, yet on my wedding day it didn't seem natural to me for Mum to be close. She didn't know how to act around me during situations like this and nor did I with her. It was as though our relationship only existed on a practical level rather than an emotional one. I had known Cath for five years now, and felt much more at ease with her than I did with my own mother.

Mum's bad mood continued throughout the morning. She wasn't happy that her minibus arrived to take her to the church before Cath and her husband, Mike, left. I saw her get on the minibus through the window, and she was very aware that Cath and Mike stayed with me until the last minute. I can appreciate that it must hurt to watch another woman with your daughter on her wedding day, but Mum had never had that kind of relationship with me and I didn't know how to create it with her.

Dad stayed downstairs to go to the church with me

in the wedding car. As the photographer arrived and started taking pictures, I suddenly saw how false everything was. He took shots of Dad getting into the car with me, and I just felt awkward being photographed with him. I had expected everything to run smoothly, to feel perfect, but I realised too late how false this day was.

We drove to the church in silence. I didn't know what to say to him. I imagined how other girls must feel on their big day, probably cuddling up to their dads, feeling loved and secure.

As we arrived at the church, the vicar came out to greet us. He explained how the music would start and then Dad and I would make our way down the aisle with the bridesmaid, flower girls and page boy behind us. As the music began, I tentatively held Dad's arm without looking at him.

But as I saw Jon standing at the altar, I realised why I was there. He looked stunning, with his blue eyes deepened by his deep blue waistcoat. He smiled at me and everything else faded away. He was the reason I was there and, with him at my side, everything made sense.

As we made our vows to one another, my heart swelled. I had always wondered what it would feel like to get married. Would I have doubts? How would I know if this was the right man? With Jon – I just knew. It 'felt' right, and that was all that mattered.

The journey back to the hotel was the complete opposite of the journey to the church. Jon and I each had a glass of champagne, and I was happy and content to be cuddling up to my husband. Being Mrs Latchem-Smith was going to take some getting used to, but I loved the sound of it. Most of all I was pleased to be able to wash my hands of my former name.

The photographer took his shots, although the pictures by now meant nothing to Jon and me. His mum and brother were not in his family shots, and the presence of my father in mine tainted everything. In the end, we didn't even collect our pictures from the photographer after the wedding. We knew the secrets behind each of the painted smiles and they were something we wanted to forget. Our own personal reminders of our day were in the memories we chose to hold on to.

Mum and Dad weren't on the top table, and Dad wasn't invited to give a speech.

I am sure that many of our guests thought us unconventional, but we didn't care. Our day had been marred by my father's involvement, and we were determined to enjoy the evening without any further unpleasantness. We stayed up dancing until late, relishing every last moment of a wonderful party. We fell into bed in a heap, overcome by the day. We were husband and wife, and nothing could come between us now.

12
That Call

Newly married and fully committed to our relationship, we decided to make our first house purchase. The new house, just outside Swansea, soon felt like home but my abusive childhood continued to taint our life. It tarnished the cosy environment we had worked so hard to create. My past was impossible to escape. It came between us every time I thought it had finally been laid to rest. I couldn't understand why Jon couldn't just let it go and move on. He, on the other hand, couldn't understand how I could. Our lives seemed to be a constant uphill struggle, and at the heart of all the conflict was my family. Every time the phone rang my heart would be in my mouth. I knew that if it was them it would create an atmosphere. Before the wedding Jon had tolerated my behaviour and just about tolerated my parents, but now that we were married he could no longer hide his distaste for them.

The fact we had two daughters played a huge part in

his increasingly inflexible attitude. He wanted no contact with my family whatsoever and, during arguments, would frequently demand that I choose between him and them. They were the source of all disagreements between us. Other than my parents there was nothing that could break us, nothing we couldn't handle together. I had done so much to build a new life but, with regard to my family, I had not progressed mentally or emotionally. I preferred to remain in my tight, safe cocoon, where I felt secure from the truth.

One evening we had an almighty row, the worst we had ever had. We had only been married a few months, yet I threw my wedding ring at Jon in despair. I couldn't take any more and neither could he. We had been going round in circles for years now. Jon wanted nothing to do with my parents. I desperately wanted them in my life. We couldn't see a way out of the stalemate. We were both too stubborn to find a middle way.

We slept on the argument, and by the morning had decided to ignore the problem once again, resuming what had become our normality – brushing it under the carpet in my family's usual fashion. It was ironic really. All my childhood I had hated my mother for ignoring the truth, ignoring what had happened to me, pretending everything was OK. Now, thirteen years later, I was doing exactly the same thing.

By this point I had even begun to doubt my own sanity. Everyone had always said that I was a liar, that I was ill and needed help. As I was growing up, my parents had tended to roll their eyes at things I said. It was a family joke that 'Julia exaggerates', and comments like this had been commonplace. What if they were right? What if it was all in my head and nothing had ever happened? I had no proof, nothing to show that the memories I had were real. How could I trust the fragmented recollections of a tormented child rather than well-trusted and respected adults who swore that nothing had ever happened?

That concept was too painful even to contemplate. If I faced my childhood head on I either had to accept that my mind was damaged and I really did need help, or that I did indeed have sick and perverse parents. Both alternatives were too awful to consider, and would have burst the utopian bubble I was living in. It was easier for me to sit on the fence and not take either road. Staying still, I at least believed I had some control over my destination.

I decided to change my hours to part time so that I could spend some more time with the girls. One afternoon Katelyn had just gone down for her nap when the phone rang. It was Dad. This in itself was not unusual – we spoke most days. However, he sounded very anxious and nothing like his usual self. I asked where Mum was, to which he replied that she was at the hairdressers. He told me how he had started going to church every week, that he was a Christian and that his religion was important to him. This was extremely unusual for my father. My brothers and I had been christened but we had never been a particularly religious family and the only time any of us had stepped inside a church in years was to attend my wedding.

'There's something I need to say to you,' Dad said. 'I know that you haven't had an easy life, and I want you to know that I know it's my fault.'

'What do you mean?' I asked. 'What are you trying to say, Dad?'

'Everything that happened when you were little, I want you to know that it did happen, and I'm truly sorry for what I've put you through. I don't want you to blame yourself,' he replied.

Suddenly my skin became clammy and my heart rate increased. I could hear it beating inside my chest. I almost dropped the phone. I couldn't believe what I was hearing. I didn't know what to say, how to react. This was something I hadn't prepared for. I had never expected this day to arrive, and now that it had I wasn't sure if I could handle the consequences. I had to know what he was admitting to. Was he telling me that every little detail that had etched itself inside my mind was the truth, that I wasn't going mad?

'You mean you did all those things, Dad? I'm not going crazy? I need to know what you're saying.'

'Yes, it all happened, Julia. But it can never go any further than this, do you understand that? Mum, Paul and Andrew can never know this; it has to stay between us. I just wanted you to know that it did happen, so you can put it behind you once and for all and move on with your life.'

I was astounded. I couldn't believe the callous way that he seemed to assume that his confession would let him off the hook. He really thought that I could just accept what he was saying and forget it all. All I wanted to do was get off the phone. I didn't want to hear any more. I couldn't take it. But there was one question that needed answering before I could end the conversation, one that had floated around my head for the past thirteen years. Why?

'Just tell me, Dad, I need to know. Why? Why did you do it?'

He sighed wearily as my question hung in the air like a bad smell. But I was adamant that I needed a response.

'Please. If you want to make this better, just tell me.'

He coughed awkwardly, stalling for time as he

seemed to struggle to find the words, and finally said: 'I just loved you too much.'

How could I respond to that? I was engulfed by a tidal wave of guilt and shame. All I wanted to do was hate him, to resent him for what he had put me through, but he was my dad . . . I still loved him. To say that he 'loved me too much' hurt me to the core. He was playing with my emotions. He knew that I couldn't hate him for loving me. Why couldn't he have said that he didn't care, that I was just there and that he used me? I needed a reason to hate him, and I still didn't feel as though I could.

I had always dreaded that I might have to face this day, even though it meant I was being given a chance to get to the bottom of everything. As I hung up the phone I fell to the floor in a heap. I felt physically drained and exhausted, and couldn't take in the conversation at all.

But things started to make sense. Now I knew why he hadn't wanted to come to the wedding, why he hadn't wanted to give me away and make a speech. I had spent years of my life debating whether my memories were valid, and he had spent them knowing what he had done, knowing exactly what he had put me through.

A mixture of emotions washed over me. Initially I

felt relieved to know, at last, that I wasn't going mad, that everything I remembered was the truth. Then I felt happy, pleased that he had had the guts to call me. I began making excuses for him. Well . . . he hadn't had to call me, had he? He could have left me feeling confused for the rest of my life, but he hadn't, had he? Surely that made him a good person – right? I was trying to convince myself, but I really didn't know what to think.

Then came the anger. How dare he think that this made everything all right? How could he leave me in this state for thirteen years and then think one little phone call made everything better? What was I supposed to do now – pretend nothing ever happened? How could I do that when I had just had proof that he was a paedophile? But that was still the problem. I didn't have proof. One phone call meant nothing, and he knew that as much as I did. I could never prove anything that he had just said to me. My mother would never believe me and I knew that Dad wasn't about to admit our conversation to her willingly. I was as stuck as before.

When I told Jon about the conversation, he was furious. He couldn't believe that my father had the audacity to admit everything and then expect me to roll over and 'take it' like a good girl. He was belittling me, treating me like an animal rather than a daughter. Jon could see that he was keeping me at bay, that he was using me to keep my mouth shut. But I desperately tried to cling to the belief that he had acted in my best interests and tried to convince myself that I should respect him for that.

I was so damaged by this point that nothing could get through to me, and I clung to the thought that my daddy still loved me. I was still the tender age of eight when he had ripped my innocence from me. In thirteen years, despite all that had changed, emotionally I was right back there in 1989, desperate to seek this Daddy's acceptance and approval.

I closed my mind to any ulterior motives there may have been behind his call, and took my father's advice. I wanted to put what had happened behind me now and move on. The past, I told myself, didn't matter.

I took my father's revelations and put them into storage at the back of my mind. He had rocked the boat, and all I wanted – all I'd ever wanted – was normality. Life carried on as though the call had never occurred. We swept the issue under the carpet once more. Jon and I continued with our daily lives, battling with our very contrasting opinions of my parents.

I needed something else to occupy my mind, to

fill the space that my past was threatening to invade. Luckily I was offered an opportunity to move to the bank's head office in Manchester, where I would really be able to make a career for myself. Suddenly the idea of a new life had never been so appealing. Since I had moved to Wales when I was seven, life had thrown problem after problem at me. I thought that relocation would give us a fresh start. And Manchester was only a couple of hours' drive from my family. I would be able to see more of them, which really appealed to me.

I discussed the options with Jon. Since initially working for the DVLA when we moved to Swansea, he had also worked for HSBC and now worked as a broadband technical adviser for BT. BT's head office was also in Manchester, which made a transfer feasible. We decided to go for it. By August everything was in place, and we piled our belongings into the back of the car and set off for a new beginning.

However, I found it hard to adapt to Manchester. In Wales everyone was friendly, people got to know one another more easily. Making friends seemed impossible in a huge city like Manchester. The bank seemed different too. Gone was the friendly banter I had grown accustomed to and the mothering natures of the girls I had worked with. Everyone seemed to be out for themselves and I found it increasingly hard to adjust.

One morning as I arrived at my desk for work, I couldn't log into the system. I had been working there for only a matter of weeks. Every time I entered my user name and password it came up with the message 'Access Revoked'. I thought there must be an error and asked my manager to check the access codes for me. She asked me to follow her into her office. I was bewildered as to what was coming next; I couldn't begin to imagine. She shut the door and asked me to take a seat.

She explained that I had acted inappropriately towards somebody's account and that I was under disciplinary action. I stared at her, open-mouthed. I had always taken great care with my work, and acted as professionally and ethically as I could. I just couldn't imagine a situation where one of my clients had complained about me without me knowing. Surely if I had upset someone I would have noticed?

The problem was that I had opened an account for a family member, which was against the rules. The person in question had mentioned my name during a conversation with another staff member on the telephone banking line, and it had been flagged up for head office's attention that I might be committing fraud or trying to access funds through a family member. I had thought I was doing a favour by opening the account and hadn't realised that I was unable to do so. Apparently it was something I never should have done. This made sense with hindsight but I wasn't aware of that regulation at the time.

I could accept that I had made a mistake, but anything I had done was done innocently and was certainly not untoward, as was being suggested.

I felt as if the ground was slipping from beneath me once more.

I went on sick leave while the matter was being investigated, only returning to work for meetings and interviews that I was required to attend. I sank into depression. I didn't want to get up in the morning. I didn't want to wash, eat, or even see the kids. Life had no purpose and I didn't know how to pick myself back up.

Now that I was home full time, I had the space I had never allowed myself before, and that meant the resurrection of all the hurt and pain I had buried. I spent days lying in bed, going over and over my past in my mind, trying to understand what had happened and trying to come to terms with it. The turmoil overwhelmed me. I was trapped in a world of deceit, lies and cover-ups and didn't know how to begin to break free.

I carried on doing the only thing I knew. I clung to my parents. They came to visit us in Manchester more and more often, encouraging me to lift my spirits and keep fighting. The end result, as usual, was even more friction between Jon and me. It came to a peak the day Mum suggested that the girls stay with her and Dad for a while to give us a break.

The look on Jon's face said it all. My relationship with my parents was a time bomb. There was only so long before the inevitable would happen. There had to be a limit to how much Jon would take, and I suspected that that limit had finally been reached. He had persevered, patiently waiting until I was ready to deal with my past, but by this point he was beginning to wonder if I ever would. However, this time, instead of the usual falling-out, tears and arguments, we sat down and discussed our relationship calmly.

'Julia, I love you,' he told me. 'But I can't do this any more. I can't stand by and condone our girls having contact with your family. You have to choose what you want from life. What's more important to you, me or them? It's not going to work, trying to have us both.'

I knew that every word he spoke was true. We were hurting each other. I considered the options he had laid out for me. How could I choose? If I chose Jon I lost everyone in my family. If I stopped contact with them I lost both my brothers and my extended family too. At twenty-two years old I wasn't sure if I felt strong enough to do that. What if Jon turned round and left me anyway? I'd be left with nobody. I walked out of the room in tears, telling Jon I needed time to clear my head and think things through. He nodded silently, hurt that it was a decision I needed even to contemplate.

I went downstairs and did the only thing I knew. I called my parents. Dad answered the phone, anxious to know why I was crying. Since the call from him the previous year, we hadn't discussed my past again but he knew that it played a major part in my marriage. Jon had always made it quite clear that he had no time for my father, and it didn't take a genius to work out why. I told him how I thought we were going to split up, that Jon couldn't take much more.

Maybe his conscience kicked in, or maybe he didn't want me back in their lives. Either way, he persuaded me to try to make a go of it with Jon. He suggested that we booked an appointment for some marriage guidance counselling, so that we could talk through our problems. I thought that if a counsellor could persuade Jon that it was unreasonable for me to cut my parents out of my life, that he was being irrational expecting me never to speak to them again, then I could win the battle without the need to choose between Jon and my family.

Neither Jon nor I wanted to end our marriage but we did know that it was at breaking point and we fervently hoped that counselling might help us find a solution. I called Relate the next morning and made an emergency appointment.

I asked my mum if she would come and baby-sit Molly and Katelyn so that we could attend. That Friday, Mum and Dad arrived from York. The girls were already bathed and in bed, and they settled down to watch TV until we returned. As Jon and I walked out of the door, I knew that this was our last chance, our only hope of making our marriage work. I hoped that the counsellor could bring Jon round to my way of thinking.

It was Jon who outlined our situation to the counsellor. He explained my history, the abuse, the way we lived now, and the sequence of events that was leading to the breakdown of our marriage. The counsellor listened intently, nodding every so often to show his understanding. In conclusion, Jon explained how he now wanted me to choose between him and my parents, and that that was the dilemma that brought us to him that day.

I sat there quite satisfied. This was the part that I had been looking forward to. Surely now the counsellor would explain to Jon how unreasonable he was being, how it was unfair of him to make me turn my back on my family.

The counsellor suddenly turned to me. 'Where are your daughters now, Julia?'

Confused by his question, I hesitated. 'At home,' I replied, wondering where this was heading.

'Right,' he answered. 'And who, may I ask, is with them?'

Jon hung his head as I replied quite confidently, 'With my parents, but it's OK – my mum is there too. It's not like I've left them alone with my dad.'

The counsellor's silence spoke volumes as I contemplated what I had just said.

'And I suppose your mum was never around when your father abused you?' he asked.

It was as if my eyes had opened for the first time. I broke down in tears as it dawned on me what I had done. My two baby girls were lying in their beds with a paedophile in the front room and I had put him there. I looked at Jon, distraught, suddenly experiencing every emotion that he must have endured for the past six years of our relationship. He looked back at me with tears streaming down his cheeks. What had I done?

What was I doing to him? What was I putting my kids through?

I felt more ashamed and guilty than I had ever felt in my life, hated myself for taking so long to see my parents for who they really were – a paedophile and a mother so obsessive she failed to witness her daughter's abuse. I had longed for the perfect life, and had created the perfect parents in my head. In reality I had put my own daughters in danger by exposing them to contact with my father, and I had never given it a second's thought. Not once had it ever occurred to me that if my father had been capable of abusing his eight-year-old daughter that he might still be capable of abusing his baby grandchildren. I had always assumed it was just me who had invited his unwanted attention.

I began to see that the fault was all his. I had never truly understood before why Jon got so upset about my family's involvement in our lives, especially after the girls had been born. Suddenly things started to make sense and I could see clearly for the first time. I felt such a failure as a mother. I was no better than my own mum, whose blinkered behaviour had let me down so badly when I had needed her the most. Thankfully, I still had a chance. I could still try to make this right.

The counsellor could see my transformation taking place before him. The reality of the situation hit me hard, especially when he explained that he couldn't continue with our sessions under the present circumstances. He told us that we were effectively putting our children in grave danger in order to see him. His words hit me like a slap in the face. But we didn't need to see him again; he had done more for me in one hour than any other person had in twenty-two years.

As we left his office I clung to Jon in desperation. I begged him to forgive me, and asked him to drive home as quickly as possible so that I could get Dad away from my kids.

Back home, I couldn't even look my parents in the eye. I was so ashamed at leaving them with my girls. For the first time in as long as I could remember, the mere sight of my dad disgusted me. I viewed them both now in a completely different light. The idyllic image I had created of them had gone, shattered by grim reality. He was no longer my dad. I couldn't change the fact that he was my father, but 'dad' was a title he was no longer worthy of. All I could see was a perverted old man who molested little girls and I wanted him to get out of my home. My mother, despite not being responsible for my father's abuse, had chosen to believe him over me. I couldn't help but feel angry and hurt for her inability to see the truth.

They must have felt our hostility, though probably didn't realise it was directed at them. We hardly said a thing and they quickly left, no questions asked. I ran into the girls' room and, thankfully, they were both sleeping peacefully in their beds. It broke my heart to see them. They were so young and vulnerable. The extreme danger I had put them in dawned on me. I silently promised them there and then that they would never be put at risk again. Never again would they be exposed to grandparents who, I now realised, were unsuitable to care for them.

I looked at Jon in a new light. He had stood by me for years, and I now understood what a hard and painful journey he had been on. I sat down at his side and begged him to forgive me. All these years I had hidden from the truth, desperate to avoid confronting my past. That night, the cocoon I had wrapped myself in had well and truly broken. There was no going back for me now. I realised the true extent and severity of what my father had done and knew that I had to do something about it.

I had spent too many years waiting for what I felt life owed me. I knew now that I had to come into my own, take control and lay the little girl inside of me to rest.

This was no longer her secret to keep. The burden was no longer hers to carry. For the first time, I became the woman I wanted to be: not my parents' daughter, but a wife and the mother of two daughters. I now had to use this opportunity to mature and develop. It was my time to spread my wings and fly to freedom.

13
Take Two

The next morning I awoke with a sense of foreboding. I knew that my life had changed for the good, that there was no going back, and yet I still had no proper comprehension of what the future held. I felt lost, unsure what direction to take next, yet strangely empowered because that was now my decision to make. I no longer had to ask my parents' permission, seek their approval. Now that my eyes had been opened to the reality of my parents' actions, for the first time I could stand on my own two feet.

Jon and I became united in our pledge to seek justice and began discussing ways to try to right the situation.

After six long years, Jon and I were finally on the same side. The one obstacle that had always come between us had gone. We were united in our decision at long last to expose the family secret that had overshadowed our entire relationship. I now knew that my father's acknowledgement of the abuse was not enough if Jon and I were to grow as a couple, especially as my father had insisted that it remain our little secret. My father assumed that now he'd acknowledged his past behaviour I would be able to move on and forgive him. He was wrong. It wasn't that simple.

Jon and I sat down that very night to discuss the situation. Jon was more focused on complete exposure; on showing my father's true colours to the world. I wanted to try to salvage some of the family I still had left. I hoped to be able to get through to my mother, to make her acknowledge what my father was capable of and what he had subjected her daughter to. If she accepted what my father had done, that also meant confronting her own behaviour, which was something I wasn't sure she would ever be capable of.

Jon commented on how much easier it would be to cope with the situation if we had recorded the conversation I had had with my father the previous year. If we had some kind of tangible proof then, surely, this time no amount of denial on his part or my mother's could prevent the whole family from finally acknowledging what had really gone on.

This was something we had discussed before. I had never had any acknowledgement from anyone in authority, even as an adult, that I was anything other than the 'girl who made up lies about her father'. To have that conversation on tape would have given me the leverage I needed to secure the trust of people around me when the time came to confront my past formally. Now that I was finally ready for that confrontation, the thing I most needed was some hard evidence.

I turned to Jon. 'Let's do it again,' I said.

My parents had no idea that I was dealing with issues from my past. They were aware that Jon disliked them, but as far as they were concerned I was the dutiful daughter who remained loyal to them. They certainly had no idea that I now wanted to expose my father's abuse. If only we could recreate the telephone conversation from last year without Dad suspecting that it was being recorded for use against him. It was essential to act fast. We only had a short period in which to achieve our goal before our change in attitude towards my parents was noticed.

We decided to go to the local police station for some advice. I still wasn't sure how far I was prepared to go but thought that it was appropriate to know where we stood in the eyes of the law before we took any action.

As we entered the police station, I felt physically sick. The familiar feelings of fear and panic arose inside me, but this time it was different. This time I was in control. There was nobody telling me what to do, what to say.

And I wasn't afraid of the consequences. This time I could dictate what I wanted to happen.

We asked to speak to someone regarding a case of historical child abuse. We were met with looks of curiosity, and the officer asked us to take a seat. After a few moments, a female officer beckoned us through to an interview room. I was anxious to ensure that the officer understood we were not, as yet, making a complaint. We just wanted some advice before we took things any further. I gave a brief overview of my childhood, explaining about the conversation I had had with my father in which he had confessed to sexually abusing me as a child. I asked her if, had I recorded that conversation, it would have been enough evidence for him to be convicted – if that was the path I decided to take.

The officer left the room briefly to take advice from her colleagues. As I sat there, what I was actually asking began to sink in. With solid evidence, I would have the power to deal with my past in any way I saw fit. I would not have to accept being known as the 'liar' any more. I could live my life in honesty and truth, and finally put the lies and deceit that had dominated my twenty-two years behind me.

After some time, the officer returned. She didn't have a definitive answer for us, but she suspected that a tape recording might not be able to be used in court, as my father would have been unaware it was being made. Jon and I were not overly surprised, but talking through the idea had made me even more determined that it was the only way forward. I still wasn't sure that I wanted to make the tape in order to secure a conviction, but the thought of having some proof regardless, if only for my own sanity, was becoming increasingly appealing.

We bought the equipment we needed and, back at home, set it up to test it and ensure that there was no interference down the phone line. We decided that we would have to act that night, knowing that the absence of a phone call to my parents would make them suspicious.

We were anxious to get the girls to bed and asleep before I attempted to make the call, so that we could eliminate any interruptions. But how would the call work? There were so many things that could go wrong. What if my father wasn't there? What if he didn't confess? What if he couldn't talk because my mother was around? There were so many factors to take into consideration, so we tried to talk through each one. We discussed all the things that could go wrong, and how I could work around them to get a confession from him. Once we felt confident that we had thought it through, we decided to go ahead, knowing only too well that we would have just this one chance to get this right. If it all fell through, it would be even harder to try to broach the subject again. It was now or never . . .

I asked Jon to leave the room while I made the call. Despite his support and admiration for what I was trying to do, this was something I had to do by myself. It was a journey I didn't feel able to share.

I lifted the receiver and called my father's mobile, allowing it to ring just three times, as I always did, to let him know I wanted him to call me back. I stuck to the usual routine so as not to arouse suspicion. Within seconds my phone started ringing. I pressed 'record' with trembling hands, and answered his call.

Mike: 'Hello!'

Julia: 'Hiya.' I sounded as depressed as I felt.

Mike: 'Hello. What's the matter?'

I sniffed and sighed, as I prepared myself for the hardest mountain I would ever have to climb; confronting my abuser head on . . .

Julia: 'Everything.'

Mike: 'Everything? That's a huge problem, "everything".'

He sounded exasperated, almost as though he knew what was coming.

Julia: 'I know.'

Mike: 'Do you want to be more precise?'

Julia: 'Where are you? In Nan's?'

Mike: 'Yeah.'

I paused, suddenly panicking about how to confront him now I knew that he was surrounded by family. The silence became uneasy as I desperately thought of a way to make it possible for me to talk to him properly.

He was the first to break the silence, changing the subject completely.

Mike: 'Where are the kids? In bed?'

Julia: 'Yeah.'

Mike: 'Where's Jon?'

I knew that if I wanted him to confess his abuse I had to make him believe that this conversation was real. I needed him to believe it was only me who was hearing his words. He was aware that Jon had taken the day off, as he had been to a job interview, but I had to maintain the illusion that Jon was nowhere around. If he had returned to work he wouldn't usually get home until much later in the evening, so I used this fact to my advantage.

Julia: 'Work.'

Mike: 'I thought he wasn't going to work today?'

Julia: 'No, he had to say he had a doctor's appointment to get time off for the interview.'

Mike: 'Oh, I see. Did you go to your interviews?'

Julia: 'Yeah.'

Mike: 'Waste of time? Or . . .?'

Julia: 'Sorry . . .?'

Mike: 'Were they a waste of time?'

Julia: 'Yeah, I don't want the job even if they offer it to me.'

Mike: 'Ah, right, OK. What about Jon?'

Julia: 'He doesn't know. He doesn't know how it went.'

Mike: 'Ah . . . okey dokey . . . Any more news from the bank?'

Julia: 'No.'

Mike: 'No? You haven't heard from anyone in Swansea as to what's going on?'

As the account I had opened for a family member was at the Swansea branch they were assisting my new manager in Manchester with the investigation. Swansea were supporting me all the way, keeping me informed of any progress. I didn't want to talk about it. I was becoming exasperated. I desperately wanted to move things on, but wasn't sure how to broach the subject. With every question he put to me it was becoming harder and harder to turn the conversation around.

Julia: 'No, no.'

Mike: 'No?'

Julia: 'No.'

I had no intention of elaborating, despite his obviously wishing for me to. I hadn't called him regarding my disciplinary, and I suspected by now that he knew that only too well.

I sighed, interrupting him as he started to question me further.

Julia: 'Can I talk to you on your own?'

Mike: 'Yeah, sure. OK . . .'

He confirmed that he had left the room and was alone.

Julia: 'Where are you?'

Mike: 'In Nan's bedroom.'

Julia: 'Oh . . .'

I knew this wasn't ideal. My nan lived in a little two-bedroomed flat, so he still would have been within earshot of my mother, Nan and brothers. I was desperate not to miss out on a full confession.

Julia: 'Can't you go outside?'

Mike: 'Pardon?'

Julia: 'Can't you go outside?'

Mike: 'Well, no one can hear. Why?'

Julia: 'I'm just . . . I'm a nervous wreck . . .'

Mike: 'Pardon?'

Julia: 'I feel like I'm a nervous wreck.'

Mike: 'You're a nervous wreck? What's making you a nervous wreck?'

Julia: 'Everything. I just can't cope.'

Mike: 'Can't cope? Having problems with Jon?'

Julia: 'Yeah.'

Mike: 'Yeah? In what sort of . . . eh . . . what sort of problems?'

He sighed, obviously seeing the direction the conversation was headed.

Julia: 'About the past.'

Mike: 'I thought we'd sorted all that?'

Julia: 'Well, we went to Relate and it's all come up.'

Mike: 'What? That night we came, or have you been since?'

Julia: 'Sorry . . .?'

Mike: 'Have you been since, or that night we came?'

Julia: 'No, the night you came.'

Mike: 'Well, it would do, wouldn't it? I mean, the past is obviously going to. When you go to marriage guidance, as it used to be called, they are going to delve into everything that is causing a problem and that has caused a lot of problems between you and Jon, and Jon and us, and what's her name – Jean, and God knows who over the years . . .'

Julia: 'Yeah.'

Mike: 'I thought, er, I thought we'd sorted through that one.'

Julia: 'Yeah, until you start bringing it up with

a counsellor between you, it brings it all up, doesn't it?'

Mike: 'Yeah, but, er, but, er, I thought Jon had agreed that, er, there's no point keep living in the past, and bringing up the past, and worrying about the past and letting it stop you living, you know?'

Julia: 'Yeah, but he's still got to talk about how he feels rather than just, you know, pretend nothing ever happened.'

Mike: 'Mmm.'

Julia: 'I just can't move on. I just, I don't understand. I've got so many questions that I need the answer to, and I just, er, I wanna move on from it, but, there's so much that I wanna know.'

Mike: 'Is that the only problem that you've got with Jon, or is life in general . . .?'

Julia: 'No – that's the only thing. That's the only thing that could break us up. And when we started talking to the counsellor about it, and you know, he started asking me loads of questions and, I just don't understand. You know, it's easy for us to talk about it last year and you say, right, bury it, forget it. You know, forget it ever happened, but it's not as easy as that because I don't understand . . . you know . . . I needed to ask you questions . . .'

Mike: 'Mmm.'

Julia: 'Because there's so much that is just going round and round my head and until I know where I am with it all I can't let it go.'

Mike: 'This is not really what you wanted to come up again, is it?'

He laughed, making light of the situation.

Julia: 'No, but I've got to know!'

Mike: 'Got to know what?'

Julia: 'I've got loads of questions, I just, I don't understand . . . You say that you love me . . .?'

Mike: 'Mmm . . .'

Julia: 'So why have you let me take all this all these years? It doesn't make sense. If you love me and you think of me, you know, as a daughter that you want in your life, I don't understand why you've let me take the blame?'

Mike: 'There's no . . . there's no question of blame. I mean blame isn't something that comes into it.'

I began crying.

Julia: 'Yes it is. 'Cause you've let everyone think that I'm some psychotic daughter who makes up lies! And I just don't understand. I can leave it in the past, but I just, I don't understand how you, you know, you say you love me and you say it all happened because you loved me too much. But if you loved me too much how can you stand by and watch me fall apart over the years the way I have?

And make out that I'm, I'm nuts, and I've made it all up, when you know I haven't . . .? I just don't understand.'

Mike: 'Well, there isn't anything else that, er, that can be said that hasn't already been said in the past, is there? It's a subject that has gone round and round and round for years, and discussed at length, and, er, you know, there isn't anything else that anybody, that anybody could say that hasn't already been said.'

Julia: 'I don't know why.'

Mike: 'Pardon?'

Julia: 'Why, why? How can you stand by and watch, watch me be like this?'

Mike: 'Er, I'm not, Julia. I mean it's not, er, it's not, er, anything that, er, I've got any control over. I mean it's, it's you and Jon, isn't it?'

Julia: 'No! I just don't understand.'

Mike: 'Well, this is, this is a subject that has been talked about to death and, and it's caused nothing but, er, unhappiness and problems with everybody.'

Julia: 'It hasn't been talked about to death at all. It's been brushed under the carpet and that's what's messed me up.'

Mike: 'Well . . .'

Julia: 'I'm a nervous wreck. I shake. I don't sleep. I can't work. I can't do anything, but it's just, er, I'm so messed up by the whole thing.'

Mike: I can't take the blame for that, Julia, I'm sorry. Every, every time that, er, there's a problem in your life or you're not coping, then, er, all you do is harp back to the past and, er, say it's my fault. You know, er, I mean, there's more to life than that.'

Julia: 'Yeah, but that's one hell of a big thing in my life!'

Mike: 'Yeah, but the past isn't, isn't responsible for the problems you've got with Co-op Bank, or, er . . .'

Julia: 'No – I'm not talking about the Co-op Bank. I'm talking about the fact that Jon can't cope with it, and I can't cope with it, and I just don't understand. I can't lay it to rest because it's just such a big issue and I just, you know, I don't know why you've, you've let me do all this? I really don't, I don't understand. I know you say you love Mum. I love Mum. And I know you say that you've just wanted to protect Mum, well I would always want to protect Mum. But in the meantime you've completely neglected me. And I'm your daughter. As well? And if you say you love me, then I just don't understand.'

By this point I was battling to control the tears streaming down my cheeks.

Julia: 'I just, it feels like I'm, you know, you've . . . you've just stood back and let everybody think that I'm some bitch from hell, and I don't know why.'

Mike: 'Well, I don't know anybody that thinks that of you.'

Julia: 'Yes you do! Because everybody thinks I've made it up and, you know, I haven't!'

Mike: 'Julia, there's . . . I don't even see that there's any mileage in you going over and over the same things over and over again, there isn't really anything left to say.'

Julia: 'Yeah, but you're the only one I can talk to. It's easy for Jon to sit by and talk to me and, you know, he's got nothing to do with it. And I can't talk to Mum, obviously. She's not well, anyway. I wouldn't put her through it.'

Mike: 'Well, you are by talking to me.'

Julia: 'Sorry . . .?'

Mike: 'I said you are indirectly, by talking to me.'

Julia: 'How's that?'

Mike: 'Well, because she's obviously gonna want to know why I've had to leave the room and talk to you, isn't she? Instead of . . .'

Julia: 'But you'll never talk to me . . .? You know? I don't know how you can just pretend that nothing's ever happened. It's so hard for me. I don't sleep at night. I just, I don't understand. I don't, I don't understand *why* in the first place. I don't, I don't understand and I need to understand, otherwise I can't put it behind me.'

Mike: 'Well, I don't honestly know how to answer your questions.'

Julia: 'Well, why did you do it?'

Mike: 'Do what?'

Julia: 'You know what!'

Mike: 'I don't, actually, Julia. I mean, er, over the course of years, erm, this subject has grown and grown like toxic and, er, has got to the stage where, er, you know, if, er, even, even I don't know what, er, what the situation is, let alone you.'

Julia: 'What, you can't remember what happened?'

Mike: 'Well, er, to listen to some of the, er, reports and, er, accounts that you have said to people over the years, it's changed and changed and changed so many times.'

Julia: 'Right! Well, you're talking to me now, not reports, and I remember everything. As clear as day.'

Mike: 'Well, I'm glad you do, yeah?'

Julia: 'How can you not? I'm the one that was the kid! If I can remember everything and it plays back and back and back in my memory then I can't imagine you can just forget about it and get on with your life.'

Mike: 'Well, it's not easy.'

Julia: 'But you don't know what I'm going through! You were the grown-up. I may be an adult now but I'm not inside, because I've never been able to move on from it.'

Mike: 'Well, I don't know how to help you with that, Julia, I honestly don't.'

Julia: 'You don't even seem sorry.'

Mike: 'Pardon?'

Julia: 'You don't even seem sorry.'

Mike. 'Well, erm, as I, er, I said just now, I mean, there's, there's nothing more that I can say that hasn't been said time and time again.'

Julia: 'You've never said anything to me . . . How am I supposed to feel? I wish I was dead. I really wish I was dead. I've got nothing to live for, because my whole life is a lie. I just wish it was all over.'

Mike: 'Well, I think you've got a hell of a lot to live for, actually. Two of them are in your bed at the moment.'

Julia: 'I tell you, they are the only things that have stopped me from ever doing anything. I just don't understand. I just wish you could be honest with me. 'Cause you're just killing me . . . I remember everything . . . and nobody else will ever know apart from Jon, but I just wish, I just wish I knew *why*. Why you've let me suffer. And why you still let me suffer. And why you don't even seem sorry for what you've put me through.'

Mike: 'I, I honestly, don't know how to, how to answer that, Julia. Because I don't think I've let you suffer at all.'

Julia: 'You don't think you've let me suffer?'

Mike: 'No, if you are suffering it's not because I've let you suffer.'

Julia: 'Excuse me? Do you remember everything that happened?'

Mike: 'No!'

Julia: 'You tried to have sex with me! You told me to take off my knickers and sit on your lap!'

Mike: 'Well . . . I don't remember that.'

Julia: 'You don't remember that!'

Mike: 'No.'

By now I was sobbing uncontrollably.

Julia: 'You must really hate me.'

Mike: 'No, I don't hate you.'

Julia: 'You must!'

Mike: 'Why?'

Julia: 'Because you're doing all this! Why, why are . . . you made me feel for years and years of my life that I was just mad, and it was all in my head, and then you say to me on the phone a year ago, that you're sorry and you only did it because you loved me too much. And, you know, to ask me to put it to rest once and for all and not tell Mum, because you could never tell her and this, that and the other. And then you can sit here and make out that you don't remember that happened, you don't remember what you did to me.'

Mike: 'I really, really don't know why this has to keep raising its head. Is it gonna happen for the rest of our lives until one of us is dead, or what?'

Julia: 'No! I just need to understand!'

Mike: 'Well, I don't understand myself so I can't help you.'

Julia: 'You don't even seem sorry, though! If you could only . . . I don't understand all this, Dad. If, if you and I could just thrash it out and understand where we both are then I can put it behind me. But you keep me on tenterhooks all the time. There's nobody else I can talk to. Nobody else was there, nobody else knows what went on, only you and me. And it's just killing me and I wanna be a mum and I wanna be a wife, and I can't because I'm so messed up over this. And I've got the counsellor sitting there at Relate saying to me, "Oh my God, how could he, you know, let you take the blame all these years?" and I'm sitting there thinking, Yeah . . . how the hell did he? How the hell did he? For somebody who loves me so much, for somebody who adored his daughter . . . how have you done this to me? I don't understand. I can understand you loving Mum, 'cause I love Mum, I'd die for Mum.

But, I just don't understand, I don't understand you. I mean, if I die by a bus tomorrow, I don't know how you live with yourself over this and I just want you to explain to me, because I love you. You're my dad. But I can't move on until it's clear in my head what the hell is going on.'

Mike: 'Well, I don't know myself, Julia, so I don't know how to. I don't know how to clear your head, when I don't understand what's in your head.'

Julia: 'Dad. I don't believe for a second that you don't remember what happened. The amount of times that you've touched me, the amount of times that, you know, things went on. I don't believe that you don't remember, and I don't understand why you're trying to hurt me further by making out you don't.'

Mike: 'I'm not trying to hurt you—'

Julia: 'Yes, you are! 'Cause there's no way that you cannot believe and, if so, then it's true what Jon says. Jon has said to me in counselling that he doesn't want you to see the girls, because he doesn't think that you're mentally stable enough to accept what you've done not to do it in the future. And I sat there in Relate and I said again and again, "No, we talked about it last year. He knows what he's done. He'd never do it again." But if you can say to me on the phone you can't even remember what you've done, how do I know my kids are safe? I'm a mother now . . . now you neglected me all these years, I can't do that to my children.'

Mike: 'Look, I can't cut through that rationalisation, I'm afraid.'

Julia: 'How can you not? If you don't know what you've done in the past, how are you gonna know what you do in the future? If you can do all those different things to me, and I can tell you, I remember each and every one . . . vividly . . . to the detail . . . it's never left me and it never will. And I have nightmares about it. But if you don't know what you've done to me, then I can't trust you around my girls.'

Mike: 'Fine, if that's the way you feel, I can't . . . You are one hundred per cent totally wrong and on a totally different planet than what you should be.'

Julia: 'Then how the hell have you admitted all this to me last year? Tell me that? How could you ring me last year, that phone call, and say to me on the phone that you were sorry, and oh my God . . . All the different things you said, and you only did it because you loved me so much, and . . .'

Mike: 'So what is the point in having this conversation again today?'

Julia: 'Because I don't understand *why*. I don't understand why you've let me suffer. I don't understand why you did it in the first place.'

Mike: 'I really do not know how to answer that, Julia.'

Julia: 'It's quite simple.'

Mike: 'It isn't, unfortunately.'

Julia: 'Yes, it is.'

Mike: 'It's . . . It's . . . It's very, very complex.'

Julia: 'Well, if you can tell me everything last year, that you're sorry, how can you suddenly forget everything you've done? In the space of months?'

Mike: 'I don't know what to say to you, Julia, I really don't. A hell of a lot happens in life, and a hell of a lot has happened in life over the last ten years, and, er, you know, it's, this . . . this has been something which has been festering in your head for years and years and years, and has grown out of all proportion, and er—'

Julia: 'No . . . no. You're not going to do this to me again.'

Mike: 'No, no, listen to me. The past is something which we have all tried to put behind us and tried to get on with life, and it's not something that occupies our thoughts, you know, twenty-four hours a day, because we've got enough current things that have caused us problems with Nan and Andrew and Mum's health, and so on.'

Julia: 'Yeah, just obviously not me.'

Mike: 'So your thoughts and views and ours have

diverted apart over the years, and so we're seeing things from a totally different angle.'

Julia: 'I don't understand why you're doing this to me.'

Mike: 'I'm not doing anything to you.'

Julia: 'You are!'

Mike: 'No, in your head I am.'

Julia: 'Then why did you say what happened to me last year? Tell me!'

Mike: 'Look, I've made it quite clear to you, more than once, that if anything I've ever said or done has caused the problems you've got now then I truly am sorry. I've put that in writing, I've said it on the telephone.'

Julia: 'Oh, yeah, all for everybody else's benefit. Please, Dad, you're talking to me now. I'm not some little kid any more that you can just wind round your little finger.'

Mike: 'I never have tried to.'

Julia: 'But how can you not remember everything you've done to me? You tried to have sex with me! You, oh my God, I'm ashamed to even say . . . All the things you've done to me. And you'd rather just let me carry on my life making me feel this desperate instead of just talking it through with me and then letting it rest. Why? I don't understand? It doesn't matter what counselling I go to . . .'

Mike: 'Because I can't honestly see any one thing I can say that is gonna make the slightest bit of difference to you and Jon.'

Julia: 'Because I can't put it behind me until we've discussed it.'

Mike: 'Well . . .'

Julia: 'Because you're making me feel mad, and I know I'm not. I remember everything with such clarity.'

Mike: 'Well, having got to the stage we're at now I can't quite see where you're trying to get at.'

Julia: 'Dad – go outside. 'Cause if you're talking like this just in case somebody overhears you, go outside. 'Cause I'm telling you what. If this conversation carries on the way it is I will never, ever see any of you again and if you wanna live your life knowing that I've lost my mum because of this, I can't cope with that and I hope to God you can because I wouldn't be able to live my life like it.'

Mike: 'This mobile phone is practically dead. I'm down to about half a bar, so it's going to conk out in a couple of minutes anyway.'

Julia: 'Go outside, then.'

He sighed and whispered to my mother that he would be back in a moment. He then confirmed he was outside.

Julia: 'Right.'

Mike: 'The phone is going to die very quickly, I think, so—'

Julia: 'Right. Just talk straight with me, because I can't live like this.'

Mike: 'Right, what do you want me to say?'

Julia: 'How could you let me live all these years feeling like this? Without ever talking to me? Why did you let everyone think I was mad? I've nearly lost Paul, I've nearly lost Mum, and I've sacrificed everything to protect you.'

Mike: 'Well, in all honesty I don't think I've . . . if I have, it certainly hasn't been intentional to let anybody think that you're mad.'

Julia: 'Well, you've never admitted it, though, have you?'

Mike: 'Well, of course not. What do you expect me to do? Sit down in front of all my family, and say, "Yes – I sexually abused my daughter!" Andrew would have no father because your mother would divorce me straight away, and she can't look after Andrew on her own, she hasn't got the health or the strength. I mean what on earth do you expect me to do?'

Andrew was still only twelve and with his developmental difficulties, he still needed full-time attention.

Julia: 'I'm not going to tell her, OK, because no one

would ever believe me anyway, Dad. You know that and I know that. I'm not dull.'

Mike: 'Well, then, what is the point of this conversation?'

Julia: 'Because, you've let me feel this way. Why have you never got on the phone to me and said, "Julia, I did, I sexually abused you", and make me feel like I'm not mad? Why have you not done that? 'Cause you say you love me, how can you let me feel like this? I don't understand, Dad.'

Mike: 'In all honesty, if you're turning around and saying to me that you remember everything that was done, you don't need me to get on the phone and say, "Yes, I did this or yes, I did that," because you know it anyway.'

Julia: 'No, but I need to hear you say it. Don't you understand that?'

Mike: 'Well . . .'

Julia: 'Because you've let me feel like I'm completely the psycho person in the family, and I've felt like absolute hell. I've been to hell and back.'

Mike: 'I thought when I phoned you last year that's what we did.'

Julia: 'I don't know how to put this behind me, but I want to.'

Mike: 'I don't know how to . . . There's no way I can

sit down in front of Mum, Paul, Andrew, Nan, anybody in the family and say that I sexually abused you when you were younger.'

Julia: 'But you did!'

Mike: 'I know. But I can't say that in front of anybody else, can I?'

Julia: 'I'm not asking you to, but I just need to hear you say it to me! To hear you acknowledge what I've been through. Because in all this, you're not the victim – I am. I'm the one who's been to hell and back.'

Mike: 'Yeah, I know, and I know it's my fault. And I think about it every single day, and I told you this a year ago.'

Julia: 'I wanna hear you say it to me.'

Mike: 'I've just said it to you now.'

Julia: 'What?'

Mike: 'That I know everything is my fault.'

Julia: 'You agree you sexually abused me?'

Mike: 'Yes.'

Julia: 'Thank you. That's all I've ever wanted all these years.'

Mike: 'But I said that to you a year ago.'

Julia: 'Yeah, but I've been through hell in Relate, and Jon's upset, and it hurts me, and it's just . . . I'm just gonna have to go through counselling and get my head around it once and for all.'

Mike: 'I mean, I feel, I know you can't put yourself in my situation, and I don't expect you to, but it's incredibly, incredibly hard for me. It has been for years. Knowing that I've upset you and put you through problems but knowing that I've got to keep up a front for the sake of the family, I mean it . . . I'm pretty certain Mum would have a stroke or a heart attack if . . . if I had to say that in front of Mum or you said it to Mum . . .'

Julia: 'She'd never believe me, Dad, I know . . .'

Mike: 'She would, she would . . .'

Julia: 'She wouldn't . . .'

Mike: 'I know Mum better than you, OK. She wouldn't . . . she could never live with me. Andrew can't cope without two parents. Mum can't look after Andrew.'

Julia: 'I know all that, but it's just, sometimes . . . And I know you did a year ago, but it seemed so brief, that conversation, that I was just so shocked that I couldn't take it in, and it's just really important sometimes to have acknowledgement.'

Mike: 'Yeah . . .'

Julia: 'Do you know what I mean?'

Mike: 'Yeah.'

Julia: ' 'Cause I've lived practically my whole life in hell. OK? I've had good days. I've had good years. But it's always there. You know? At the back of my mind, and I've just . . . I've lived years thinking, oh my God . . . you know . . . what's wrong with me?'

Mike: 'No . . . I mean, I take full responsibility for it and I have done internally all these years.'

Julia: 'I'm not trying to put you through hell again. It's just . . . you've got to understand how I feel.'

Mike: 'I know, but, erm . . . you know . . . it's just got to be you and me. It's the only way it can be.'

Julia: 'I know.'

Mike: 'There's just too much going on in the family with illnesses and problems, and, er, it doesn't work if we go down that road again.'

Julia: 'I know.'

Mike: 'But, you know, I've never stopped feeling guilty for all the problems that I've caused.'

Julia: 'Yeah?'

Mike: 'I mean, I don't sleep, I wake up every night and you're always on my mind and the problems are always on my mind.'

Julia: 'I'm not trying to cause that, I'm not . . .'

Mike: 'I know you're not. I know you're not. But, erm, it's the way it's got to be. But, er . . .'

Julia: 'I know that. It's just that I've spent so many years blaming myself, hating myself. I feel so . . . I feel such a cow . . . I've got a problem in my relationship with Jon 'cause I just . . . I can't think like that . . . it's just completely ruined me. It's destroyed me inside out, and I've needed you just to get on the phone and say, "Julia, you're not mad, it happened, I know it happened and it's not you." '

Mike: 'I thought I did this last December?'

Julia: 'I know, but it was such a shock to hear somebody say after all those years that I wasn't mad, that I just couldn't take it in. I went into shock then. I came off the phone and I was just lying on the floor shaking, because I just . . . to suddenly have somebody tell you that you're not mad, it's such a release.'

Mike: 'Well, I've said it again now, OK!'

He said it with a laugh.

Julia: 'Right, I'm just gonna have to go to counselling and sort myself out.'

Mike: 'Yeah, okey dokey.'

Julia: 'All right, you better go back in. Tell Mum I've had a row with Jon, or something.'

Mike: 'Well, no, she's obviously gonna know that it's the past resurrecting itself. I will just have to try and word it sensibly.'

He continued laughing.

Julia: 'Mmm.'

Mike: ' 'Cause Nan doesn't know what's going on, and, er, Mum gets really uptight, then Andrew picks it up and Paul picks it up and then, you know. The doctor wants to get Mum on to beta-blockers but, erm, her blood pressure has been through the roof for two years, even on pills, you know? I have all these things to worry about as well.'

Julia: 'I know, and I feel guilty for most of it.'

Mike: 'No, no, it's not your fault!'

Julia: 'No – but I do, because Mum's not been right since everything happened back then.'

Mike: 'Yeah, but whose fault is it ultimately? Mine.'

Julia: 'Yeah.'

Mike: 'I mean, you talk about guilt. I mean, the amount of guilt I carry around with me is unbelievable.'

Julia: 'The biggest thing, right, I can understand Mum because Mum adores you and in her mind you are like her perfect man and everything, and I'm not trying to disillusion that. It's Paul. Right? Because Paul and I are really close, and he has told me on numerous occasions that, well, that I need a psychiatrist basically, because I've got a problem with all the things I've made up and, you know, he doesn't trust me. And that hurts, because I adore Paul. And I would do anything to have him closer, but he thinks, you know . . . He's always got that edge to him around me.'

Mike: 'He loves you.'

Julia: 'I know he does, but . . .'

Mike: 'He's always talking about you.'

Julia: 'I know . . .'

Mike: 'Oh! It's a funny old life, isn't it!'

He laughed . . . belittling the situation completely.

Julia: 'Go on, you better go. Jon will be in soon . . .'

Mike: 'Bye!'

Julia: 'Bye.'

14
Yorkshire Tales

I hung up the receiver and fell to the floor. Jon came rushing in and held me tight as I sobbed in his arms. I'd done it, I had his confession and nothing could ever take that away from me. I felt emotionally and physically drained. I could never have imagined how hard it was going to be to obtain his admission, and it was by far the most gruelling thing I had ever had done. Thankfully my perseverance had paid off. There had been times during the conversation that it felt pointless, that I wasn't getting anywhere close to the confession I so needed, but eventually he had given in and given me the evidence I wanted.

My exhaustion soon lifted as the power I now held began to sink in. Excitement began to rise inside me, and I turned to Jon in absolute elation.

'Oh, my God, we've done it! That's it. It's over now, isn't it?'

He smiled back at me with absolute pride. 'Yeah, babe, it's over,' he confirmed.

I would never again have to pretend that nothing had ever happened for fear that I wouldn't be believed. I had hard evidence.

'What do you want to do with it?' Jon asked me.

I really didn't know. We had the power to do anything, play the tape to anyone and expose Dad for what he really was – a child molester.

'I want to go to Paul.'

I was desperate to make clear to Paul that I wasn't the troublemaker the family had always made me out to be. I knew he would stand by me, trust me and take care of me, whatever consequences I would have to face. Ever since we had worked together as teenagers there had been a special bond between us, and I needed him now more than before. He would even call me and ask my advice about girlfriends; I had never stopped adoring him, despite knowing that he deep down believed Mum and Dad's opinion of me to be correct. I was desperate to prove otherwise. We decided to make the journey to York the next day, and play Paul the conversation we had taped. I thought that Jon, Paul and I could decide together how best to proceed with the tape.

Sitting in the car, I felt a mixture of anxiety and excitement. This was my time, the day I had been waiting for, for most of my life. I wondered what Paul's reaction would be. Would he want to go straight to the police? Would he want to hurt my father? I couldn't imagine what he would do first when he learned what his little sister had suffered. I was glad Jon was with me to help. He would be in a calmer frame of mind to talk Paul through things if it was too much for him to take in.

I had called Paul on the way to let him know we were coming. He was surprised but accepted that I would explain everything on arrival. He probably imagined I was going to tell him I was pregnant again. I don't think anything could have prepared him for the shock he was about to get. As we pulled up outside Paul's house, Jon and I exchanged reassuring looks. We knocked on the front door, and Paul answered it with a smile.

'Come in!' He gestured towards the living room and we settled the girls on the sofa. Paul lived with a housemate from university, so I asked Jon to look after the girls while I went upstairs to talk to Paul.

Paul looked nervous. He seemed completely baffled as to why I would make the journey to York, needing to speak to him so privately. I looked at him and, with a sigh, sat on his bed. I took a deep breath.

'Paul, there's something I need to tell you . . .'

'Go on,' he replied.

'You know all the problems from the past, the things I said happened with Dad? It was all true, Paul. It did really happen, but I knew no one would ever believe me. Now I've got proof.'

He stared at me, unsure how to react.

'What proof?'

'I called him last night. He confessed to the abuse, Paul, and I recorded every word. I've got it here. Just listen to it?'

Paul took the tape from my hand, walked silently across the room and put the cassette into his stereo. He pressed 'Play'.

We listened to the tape in silence. I began to cry. The emotions I had experienced during the call came flooding back. Soon Paul had tears streaming down his cheeks too, and he pulled me close. He held me tight until the tape came to an end. I looked up at him.

'Please, Paul? Please look after me? Please make this better?'

'Don't worry. I will. I'm here for you, Jules, and I'm not going to let anything ever happen to you again.'

I sobbed with absolute relief. However much I had hoped that he would stand by me, there had been a niggling doubt that he would turn his back and not want to know. I was so relieved that the pressure was off me to take control. I had Paul on my side now, and I knew that everything would be OK.

Paul stood up and began pacing the floor in despair, contemplating what to do next.

'I'm sorry, Julia, but I've got to confront him. I've got to see him face to face and make him admit to me what he's done.'

I stared at him in horror.

'No! Please, Paul! Let's deal with this together! Please don't go and see him.'

But my pleas fell on deaf ears. He picked up his phone and called my father.

'Dad, I need to see you. Come and meet me now, outside Sainsbury's.'

My father must have agreed as Paul hung up the phone and reached for his coat. I felt heartbroken. I begged him not to go, not to leave me there. But he just hugged me once more, promising to return as soon as possible. I followed him downstairs, and sat with Jon on the sofa. The front door slammed behind my brother.

Jon looked bewildered. 'What happened?' he asked.

I explained that Paul had heard the tape and had gone to confront my father. Jon felt completely disempowered. Things were spiralling out of our control. All we could do was sit and wait for Paul's return.

About half an hour later, he came back in a

completely different frame of mind. Gone was the concerned and distraught brother, in his place was a calm, serene person I did not recognise.

'Julia, Dad's outside. He wants to talk to you,' he said.

'No way!' I shrieked. I was horrified that he could even contemplate the idea of putting us face to face. Why on earth would I want to speak to Dad? He now knew that I had recorded our conversation from the day before. But Paul begged me to speak to him.

'Please, Julia, for me? I will come with you. You won't be alone.'

I felt helpless to argue. I didn't know what to do for the best, how to act.

Paul led me outside to my father's car, and we sat together in the back, with my father in the driving seat. He looked weary. Sitting in that car with him, I felt eight years old all over again. It was just as it had been for the years he had subjected me to his sexual advances. I was furious with Paul for putting me in this position.

Paul confronted my father.

'Tell me the truth, Dad,' he said. 'What really happened?'

I felt so betrayed. What did he mean, what 'really' happened? Was he suggesting that my version of events was untrue, that I was making things up?

Dad confessed to touching me a few times, simply stating that yes, he had done things wrong, but it was nowhere near as 'dramatic' as I was stating, and that over time I had elaborated the story beyond all belief. He appeared sheepish as he spoke, and remained facing forwards in the car at all times whilst Paul and I sat in the back looking at the back of his head. He point-blank denied that anything else had ever happened. I became hysterical.

'How can you say that? You bastard! I hate you. Why are you doing this to me? I can't take any more!'

Paul turned to me. 'Jules, I think over the years your mind has twisted this. I'm not saying it's your fault, but I do think you need help. Dad is obviously in the wrong for the things he did do, but I can't imagine he ever would have taken it any further.'

His words felt like a stab in the back. His betrayal was the ultimate blow. I sobbed in utter despair. Nothing I said made any difference. Even with the confession. Without him admitting to each and every thing he had ever done, one by one, it wasn't enough to convince Paul. Surely it must seem strange to Paul that after years of Dad denying that 'anything' had ever happened, he was suddenly admitting to a few things? Couldn't Paul see that Dad was only admitting to the bare minimum in order to explain away the tape with as little damage to his reputation as possible? Paul seemed pleased with my father's explanation, satisfied that he didn't have to deal with a situation as bad as he had initially thought. Paul turned to my father.

'Regardless of it only being a few times, Dad, you still have to tell Mum. I can't keep this to myself.'

My father agreed to tell my mother, and Paul arranged to go with him.

'I'm coming, too,' I said defiantly. There was no way I was letting them tell her half a story. If my mother was going to hear what happened, she had to know the truth, the complete truth, not the shortened version that my father and brother had devised.

'No way,' my brother snapped. 'You're staying here. Dad and I will go alone.'

I was caught in yet another of the famous family cover-ups, powerless to intervene. All the control I had felt was mine the night before had slipped through my fingers. It had been a mistake to trust my brother. He was happy to accept the first explanation that made their lives easier, regardless of how that affected me.

Even if what my father said had been true, even if he had only ever touched me a few times, that still amounted to child abuse. Paul was accepting his actions as though he had made a little mistake, rather than admitting to being a paedophile. I returned to Jon, feeling as though my life may as well be over. Our mission to expose the truth had fallen apart in front of my eyes. What had I done wrong? How did this happen? It just didn't make sense. We had proof! Why would no one listen to us?

A couple of hours passed, and we began to wonder what on earth was happening at my parents' house. What had they told my mother? What did she say? I hated being cut out of the situation like a naughty little girl, and began to regret staying put at Paul's house as I'd been told. I was an adult. I didn't have to accept being dictated to any more. We decided to follow Paul to my parents' flat, to see for ourselves what was happening.

When we got there, Paul's girlfriend was just arriving to collect Paul. He seemed surprised to see us, but I walked straight past him and up the stairs in my parents' flat. Mum was crying. Dad was standing behind her. My first instinct was that Mum was crying for me, that she was heartbroken to discover her husband had treated her daughter in such a way. I instinctively put my arms around her, hugging her. My mother and I had never gone in for much physical contact, and I couldn't remember ever hugging her before in my life. If only she knew the rest of the story, I thought to myself, but she was so distressed I didn't think it appropriate to tell her then. I decided to let her come to terms with what she had heard, and tell her the full story the next day. I said my goodbyes to her, and gave my father a blank glare as I walked downstairs to the car. I sat down next to Jon, feeling exhausted.

'Take me home?' I asked him, and we made our way back to Manchester.

I soon realised that my mother's tears were for my father rather than for me. She called the next day and said that she didn't want any further contact with Jon and me. She had decided to stand by my father and wanted no part of the accusations I was making about him. I found this difficult to take. Naïvely I had expected that with proof she would have to listen to me. Even though he was only admitting a small part of the abuse, surely that was enough for her to realise that he had lied to her for years, and was continuing to lie to her face. Paul, sadly, felt the same way. I found this extremely hard to deal with. I had always seen him as a good, loyal person, although Jon begged to differ. He had never been close to Paul and had suspected that, when confronted with the truth, he would be happy to cover it up in accordance with my mother's wishes. He was loyal only to my parents, who didn't want any problems to interfere with their 'Victorian-style' lives, as Jon had always described it.

For years, Jon had been able to see how their regimented attitude was like that of characters in a period drama. They worked hard to maintain the illusion of respectability, with their judgements and snobbery, despite the disgrace of my father losing his job. He now worked as a shelf stacker in Marks & Spencer's. Gone was their four-bedroomed detached property, and they now lived in a two-bedroomed flat. Despite their social decline, they existed in a world of make believe, anxious to project the image of a contented and happy family. Any problems that threatened to break that image were met with disdain and denial. Even though their characters had always been right in front of my eyes, it was only now that I was seeing them in their true light.

Jon and I spent the next few days taking in the events that had transpired in York, and their aftermath. The shock of my family's reaction took time to sink in. We had to consider what options we had left. Paul begged me not to continue with any further action, asking me to leave the past where it belonged. He made me promise not to make any hasty decisions, and to think hard before I made 'any big mistakes'. I agreed to this, also not wanting to rush into anything, but made my feelings of betrayal quite clear to him. As far as I was concerned my family were no longer a necessary part of my life.

I had been dependent on their love and affection for far too long, and had lost my integrity because of it. With my hard evidence and new-found sense of security, I found that the truth really had set me free. I didn't need them in order to feel whole. In fact I felt more alive than ever without them in my life.

During this time, only a couple of months after I made the tape, the disciplinary action with the bank came to an end. I was given a warning, and asked to resume my duties. I knew that I could appeal against the decision – I had never acted maliciously or with the intention to deceive – but it was no longer an important part of my life. I had so much else to think about. I accepted their decision amicably but, for now, refused their invitation to return to work. With my mind cleared of work, it dawned on me that what had happened in my childhood wasn't about me any more. To a certain extent it didn't matter now what Dad had done to me in particular, it was what he was capable of in general that began to focus my mind and decide the course of action I would take . . .

If I didn't make a stand, what was there to stop him ever touching other kids? What about when Paul or Andrew had children of their own? Paul didn't believe our father was a paedophile and so wouldn't think twice about putting his kids at risk. I had to do something to make sure that he never hurt anybody else. Andrew, owing to his age, wasn't even aware of my past. He had been too young to realise when I had gone into care as a teenager, and had never been told anything about the situation since. I had to protect Andrew as well as my own kids . . .

I decided to report my father to the police.

That afternoon, with Jon by my side, I called Didsbury police station. I told them that I wanted to report a case of historical child abuse. They promised that an officer would be with us later that day. Jon and I sat there that evening, with the kids sleeping in their room next door, knowing that we were about to embark upon the most serious thing we had ever done. But we both felt quite calm. This was the final part of taking back our power, taking control of our lives, and making a stand against my family.

They may have been content to bury – or ignore – what Dad had done, but we were not. Somebody needed the strength to say no, it wasn't acceptable. Jon and I seemed to be the only members of my family with a moral code. No one has the right to touch a child in a sexual manner, in whatever circumstances, and with whatever so-called consent. This was something that I had come to learn over time. I had always felt, as a child that, because I let him do it, because I had even encouraged him at times, the blame lay at my door. Surely, I had thought, I had to take some responsibility if I wasn't saying no. If he had hit me, or forced me, then surely that would amount to abuse. But it had felt ambiguous that someone I loved was touching me, even though I didn't know the true meaning of what he was doing.

If we could expose him for the person he really was and save just one other child's innocence, then our actions would be worthwhile. It was people like my mother and Paul – people who won't accept what their loved ones have done, believing them incapable of an offence because they think they know them well – who let paedophiles walk our streets. My dad had already had a near miss when he was taken in for questioning when I was ten years old. That scare had not prevented him from continuing to abuse me sexually for a further three years. This to me meant that he still posed a threat to society. Jon and I were determined to put one of the country's paedophiles behind bars.

Despite the people my parents were, I still loved and cared about them both. How could I not? Love for your parents isn't something you can switch off. I had delayed facing my past for so long because of the hope that one day I would see them differently, that one day I could hate them and the love I felt for them would die. That day never came. It was up to me finally to accept that the two sides of my father that I had always managed to separate were actually the same person, and to do something about it. The man who cuddled me when I was little and took me to the park was the same man who had tried to rape me. And that realisation had hit me hard. I would never stop loving my parents, but my love didn't mean I had to accept their actions. By exposing my father's perversion, I was making the world a better place for all concerned. I felt no guilt. I had no regrets about handing Dad over to the police. It had taken me a long time to get to this stage, but now I was there I knew I was doing the right thing.

I gave my statement to the police. The two female officers listened intently as Jon and I described what had happened, everything my father had done, and the proof we had of his guilt. They made copious notes, and appeared to be baffled by how together we were. These were words I was to hear a lot over the next few years. The officers expected me to break down, to be a psychological mess after everything we had been through, but we simply felt at peace to be doing the right thing. I felt sad that life had come to this, sad that Dad had ruined his life and ruined much of mine.

I could now choose how I wanted the rest of my life to pan out. I knew that by taking this action I had lost my family for ever, but I felt strangely at peace with that decision. I didn't have to answer to them any more. I wanted to stand tall and show that I didn't accept their behaviour. I may have shared their blood, but I certainly didn't share their views and opinions. If they were unable to face the truth and do something about it, I would do it for them. There was no going back.

15

A Birthday to Remember

Now that we had made that first step of reporting my father, Jon and I wanted to move on with our lives. We went back to South Wales just after Christmas 2004.

Being back at home was the best move we could have made. Jon's dad, Mike, and stepmum, Cath, lived nearby and the girls loved being close to their paternal grandparents. But as we waited to hear back from the police, the case was like a cloud hanging over us.

During this time my family had no idea I had spoken to the police and presumed that I had taken no further action. I hadn't spoken to any of them since our trip to York, and I was happy to maintain my distance.

Manchester police referred our case to Bridgend, who in turn passed the case to Dyfed-Powys police department as the case had to be dealt with by the force covering the area in which the offences took place. This caused a delay and it was February before my official statement was taken.

Detective Robert Inkster and his partner, who worked for CID in Dyfed-Powys, came to the house. Jon and I were nervous. I knew that this was it. Once they had my official statement things would start moving, and I was anxious to discover what the next step would be. I was dreading having to disclose once more all the things that had happened, and I hoped that I could find the words.

But once settled in the living room, Rob – as we would come to know him – told us that he had found the original video interview of the disclosures I made against my father when I was in care. If I preferred, he could write my statement based on those disclosures and I could sign it. It would save me the turmoil of having to talk through the intimate details. I was grateful for this alternative. I found it difficult discussing the abuse with Jon, let alone two policemen I didn't even know.

Rob explained that he had come to the house to meet us properly as he would be the officer in charge of the case, and to give us the opportunity to ask any questions. I asked what the next steps would involve. He explained that once my statement was typed and signed, he would liaise with Yorkshire police for a convenient date for my father's arrest. Rob himself would then travel to York to question him officially. I handed

Rob the tape, asking whether it could be used in evidence. He told me he would take it with him, but it would be up to the Crown Prosecution Service (CPS) to make that decision, depending on whether or not they took the case on.

This confused me. I had assumed that the police would arrest Dad and take things further. But the fact of the matter was that if my father confessed to the accusations, then the CPS didn't need to get involved. My father would then be held in custody until sentenced by a judge. However, if he denied the accusations it would be up to the CPS to decide if the case was strong enough to go to court. It was only if we got that far that the tape's validity would be assessed.

I felt, for the first time, that somebody was being straight with me, and I valued Rob's direct approach. He left the house, promising to return the following week with the statement for me to sign. Jon and I sat down to try to take in everything we had heard. We were so pleased to be finally taken seriously.

As promised, Rob came over the next week with my statement. Reading over the words I had used in 1994 drove home how young I had been. The majority of the offences were outlined, although there were a few omissions that needed to be added. This, although necessary, further delayed the trip to York for my father's arrest. Rob promised to include the omissions and post the statement back to me for me to sign, which I diligently did immediately on receipt.

In the meantime, we tried to reintroduce some normality into our lives, and I finally resumed work for the bank. I was able to remain employed by the same company by transferring my job from the Manchester branch to Bridgend. We carried on with life, until the call came to tell us about my father's arrest.

My father's fifty-sixth birthday was 8 March 2004, a birthday he would never forget. That evening, Yorkshire police arrested him in anticipation of Rob's arrival the next day. My father was collected in the middle of the night and taken to a cell to await Rob's interrogation. On 9 March Rob interviewed my father in York police station. My father had a duty solicitor present, and apparently replied, 'No comment' to each and every question put to him. Rob could get no further response from him and, eventually, Dad was released on bail pending further inquiries. Thankfully, as a condition of his bail, he was unable to make any direct or indirect contact with me. I was safe from the manipulation I had experienced as a child. There was no way that I would be retracting this time.

Rob called me to explain what had happened during questioning. Because of Dad's 'no comment' responses, it was now up to the CPS to decide whether to take the case on. My father would remain on bail until that decision was reached. This information hit me harder than I ever could have predicted. Even now my father was making me fight for the truth. If he had any compassion he would have saved me the pain that waiting for the CPS's decision would cause me.

I asked Rob again and again how long it would take, when exactly we would be likely to hear from them, but there was no way of knowing. I needed to do something. I had to contribute. I felt useless unless I could add something to the case and, despite working full time, began researching what information about me was held on file with Social Services. I was anxious to find something that might help the police with their inquiries, something that might encourage the CPS to take my case on. I knew that if my case went ahead it would involve a crown court trial, but now that we had come this far we had to see it through. If the CPS refused my case it would be tantamount to saying that there was no substance to my allegations, that they didn't believe my father had committed the offences. I don't think anything could prepare me for such a blow and it spurred me on to seek some form of additional proof to substantiate my claims.

I managed to find Buddug Ward, the social worker

who had worked with me all those years ago. I called her, asking for her help. She told me that she had always known the truth, so confirmation of my father's abuse came as no surprise to her. She directed me to Aberaeron Social Services, where my records were likely to be held. I called them next, anxious to follow the trail. Mary Williams, another social worker who had been involved with my case as a child, took my call. She confirmed that my notes were there, and I arranged a date to go and view them.

A few weeks later I took the day off work, and went with Jon to Aberaeron. Mary showed us through to a room where my notes were laid out on a table. They were substantial, to say the least, and we began ploughing through them. We spent hours that day reading letters, reports and various entries over the years from social workers, police, psychologists, doctors and my parents.

There was even a letter from my nan saying how I was untrustworthy and prone to exaggeration. It had my parents' influence all over it, and I could practically hear them dictating the words. Sadly, over time, my nan's condition had only deteriorated, so I was unable to speak to her regarding the case. I was lucky if she was ever coherent enough to remember me, let alone comprehend the court proceedings.

Unfortunately we left that office with nothing concrete. I had been so desperate to find something, anything, but in reality I just didn't know what I was looking for. I resolved to give up and leave the investigations to the police.

Back at home I tried to fill my time. I couldn't bear the prospect of merely waiting for the CPS to make their decision, and quickly fell back into the cycle of cramming my time with as much as was humanly possible. My whole life was balancing in someone else's hands, and I hated it.

With every day that passed, I found it harder and harder to keep up with my self-inflicted hectic lifestyle. I just couldn't cope with the many pressures on me, and my mind began shutting out all intrusions in an attempt to keep sane. I became more manic than ever before, living in a state of heightened alert.

I think I suffered an undiagnosed breakdown. My mind was fragmented, and even the simplest tasks posed a problem for me. I was incapable of completing what I had started and, as a family, we were living in chaos. I stopped doing any housework – clothes weren't washed, dishes weren't done and the entire household began to fall apart as I struggled even to get out of bed in the morning. Jon tried his best to keep things going but he simply couldn't keep up with everything on his own. I quit my job at the bank and, with no reason to get up every morning, I soon rarely bothered. It was common for Jon to come home from work to find me sitting exactly where he had left me, still in pyjamas, with my unbrushed hair hanging in straggly locks around my neck.

The weeks dragged on and we still hadn't heard a word from the CPS. The stress of having our lives on hold really took its toll. I fell so far into a depression that one night I even contemplated taking my life.

I was sitting on a chair in the front room, unable to sleep. I had entered a self-destructive pattern of sleeping all day and lying awake at night, a dangerous time to contemplate life. I sat there, silently crying, unable to see a solution to the way I felt. If the CPS took the case on I would be faced with the trauma of giving evidence in court, and if they declined the case, I had lost everything. I couldn't win either way.

I walked into the kitchen, and took the anti-depressants I had been prescribed out of the cupboard. Jon had urged me to see my doctor, but when I had returned with anti-depressants he had begged me not to take them. He wanted us to work through our problems together without my growing dependent on tablets to feel alive. I poured the tablets into my hand, squeezing their cold shells in my palm. I closed my eyes and thought about what I was contemplating . . . How had my life come to this? I glanced at a picture Molly had drawn me, which I had stuck to the fridge door, and reluctantly, one by one, tipped the tablets back into the jar.

Molly and Katelyn didn't deserve that. My own parents had put me through hell. My little girls didn't deserve me doing the same to them. Suicide would have gone against everything I believed in. I was keen to have a big family, create a happy home.

Rob had offered me counselling with Victim Support, but at the time I had declined, thinking I could deal with this my own way. After that night with the tablets, I decided it might be a good idea. I didn't want to feel this way any more, and if there was even a remote possibility that Victim Support could help me out of the depressive state I was in, then it was worth a try. I called the number Rob had given me and made an appointment to go in. I found it extremely hard to trust people around me, and was on my guard with my counsellor all the time. She hardly stood a chance. At first, I felt as though she was judging me and that she didn't believe me. But, eventually, I began to let her in and allowed myself to let go emotionally and cry with her.

At her suggestion, I tried to resume some of my old hobbies. She thought that if I saw my friends more, and did the things I've always enjoyed, I would come out of myself a bit. It was destructive to stay home alone every day.

It was at this time, in early 2004, that I met a woman called Yvonne Bailey – a lifestyle coach. She was a similar age to my mother, and she took me under her wing. We soon became firm friends, and she offered me the emotional support I so desperately needed from a mother figure, which was lacking in my life. She was full of what I call 'tough love'. She didn't pander to me, pity me, or allow me to wallow in self-pity. She made me wake up and listen to what she had to say. I was lucky – I had my health, a beautiful family that I had created for myself, life wasn't really as bad as I had first imagined. Yve was always there for me if I started to fall, pushing me back up and keeping me mentally on track. She was exactly the sort of person I needed in my life at that point, and she became a tower of strength for both Jon and myself. The burden of responsibility was lifted from Jon's shoulders a little, which allowed us to help each other through the proceedings. I began to realise that I had depended on other people to lift me up, and keep my spirits high. Now I began to see that life could be exactly what I made it. I wasn't put on earth to be raped, abused or mistreated. That had happened as a result of my father's free will. I was here to experience things that would make me stronger, things that I could learn from and change from negative to positive.

I began to get excited about the potential my life held. I had had my fair share of hurt and betrayal, but the amount I had learned from that gave me a distinct advantage over many other people. I could really make a difference; use what I had learned to help others who were finding it hard to cope; educate people who didn't understand child abuse, who didn't understand how it affects people's lives. I pledged to seek justice, not only for myself, but for other children and adults who have been abused. I wouldn't rest until I succeeded.

This attitude gave me a new lease of life, and the motivation I needed to fight for this court case. I wasn't working for myself any more; I had the bigger picture at the forefront of my mind. I was beginning to see who the real 'Julia' was, and I decided I quite liked her. It was a voyage of self-discovery. There was no room for self-pity. I learned to look at myself in a whole new way, learned how to face my demons, and admitted to myself that I too was capable of manipulating situations. I began truly to appreciate the people who had stood by me and taken me for who I was, even when I couldn't see that person myself.

On 3 November 2004, the CPS gave their final decision. My father, Michael, was officially charged with ten counts of sexual offences against a child, and would stand trial in Swansea Crown Court.

16
Trials and Tribulations

My father was being charged with five counts of sexual assault on a child, four counts of gross indecency and one count of attempted rape. He was pleading not guilty to all ten charges, hence he had to appear in a magistrates' court in December 2004. He pleaded not guilty to the judge, who, owing to its severity, immediately passed the case to the crown court. In January 2005, my father repeated his not guilty pleas to the judge in crown court, and the case was adjourned to give both barristers time to prepare.

My father had a QC representing him, a young dynamic man who liaised with him throughout the period that we were waiting for the date of the trial. I, in contrast, had no contact from anybody. Despite the fact that I had reported the incidents, it was now the CPS who were prosecuting my father, not me. My position in the case was nothing more than a key witness for the prosecution. Nobody was allowed to discuss the case with me for fear of guiding or leading my evidence. With hindsight this makes sense but, at the time, I felt more isolated and alone than I had felt before.

Jon helped me through that difficult phase. I was still absolutely amazed that the case had reached crown court. Deep down, I suspected that, once again, I either wouldn't be believed or the lack of evidence would go against us. By strange coincidence, I had gained some knowledge of crown court procedures the previous year. I had been called to attend jury service on a case of historical child abuse. It was uncannily similar to my own.

The case concerned a young woman who had suffered abuse from her father and, as in my own case, she had waited fifteen years to report the incident. The jury agreed unanimously that her story was indeed true and her father was found guilty of all charges against him.

This knowledge had put me in good stead for my own trial. I now had some hope that despite my case being historical there was a chance that justice could still prevail. Unfortunately, we had a number of months to wait. My father had to attend various preliminary hearings. Finally, however, the date came through for the trial – 18 July 2005, a date that will stay with me for ever. As the weeks went past and July came closer, I started preparing for the inevitable ordeal. I spent hours anticipating all the questions my father's QC might put to me, thinking of all the possible things he could say. I tried very hard to prepare myself for the worst, reasoning that if I expected the most horrific experience then anything less would be a bonus.

I woke early on the Monday the trial began. The day before, we had taken the girls down to stay in Emlyn with Jon's mother, Jean, until the trial was over so the house was deathly quiet as I dressed. Jon didn't know how to act around me. I didn't want to be fussed over. I was scared of breaking my resolve if I allowed myself to experience any emotion. We collected Yve, who had agreed to come with us for moral support, and arrived in Swansea early, deciding to have breakfast and a 'pep talk' before we were due in court. I knew full well I was going to have to face my mother, father and Paul for the first time since September 2003 and the prospect terrified me. Jon kept reassuring me that I was doing the right thing and that I had nothing to be ashamed of. The only way I could cope was to keep repeating his words again and again inside my head, psyching myself up for the most traumatic event of my life.

My fear of having to see my father and mother for the first time in many months was eased a little by the court's suggestion that we used the judges' entrance at the rear of the building, so that we could avoid any early confrontation. We were shown through to the vulnerable witness unit, where we had a private waiting room and washroom. I was terribly nervous and just wanted to get on with it now, but for some reason we were left in the waiting area for what seemed like hours. I couldn't understand it. I had been told that we would be called into the courtroom to witness the jury being sworn in, but there was no sign of the clerk of the court, or Rob Inkster, for that matter.

Eventually, Rob came in, looking very serious, and asked me to sit down. He explained that my father's barrister was offering us a plea bargain. Dad would plead guilty to four charges of sexual assault if we dropped the other six charges against him. Rob suggested to us that we seriously consider his offer, pointing out that if we progressed to full trial we ran the risk of Dad being acquitted of all charges if the jury found him not guilty.

My immediate reaction was utter fury. What a bastard! This trial had been on the cards for over a year now and he had never budged from his not guilty plea on all charges. Now that he was faced with a full trial he was trying to manipulate me once more into accepting a bargain. No chance.

Rob left the room so that we could discuss my

options in private. We were surprised by my father's audacity – and bloody angry.

I couldn't change my mind, even though I knew that a partial admission of guilt was better than none at all. If I accepted my father's bargain he was once again taking control away from me. I was stronger now. I needed to tell my story once and for all, and let twelve complete strangers decide his fate. If he was found not guilty at least I would have stood my ground, given it my all. Accepting his bargain was like admitting defeat.

In the meantime, we had been told that the taped evidence was admissible in court. Rob let us know when he presented the plea bargain to us. It was going to be played in full for the jury. Suddenly my father's plea bargain made perfect sense. There was no remorse there. Now that it was certain that the evidence would be played in court, he knew once the jury heard the tape he would have some serious explaining to do. Offering to admit to the lesser charges was an easy way out for him, and one that I wasn't prepared to grant.

We were sent home to discuss the decision we had made and asked to come back on Wednesday with our final decision. As far as we were concerned our final decision had been made, but the CPS were concerned that we were rushing into the trial without considering the consequences. It seemed obvious to me that the

CPS did not agree with our decision to proceed to trial. They knew only too well how hard it was to get an historical conviction and wanted us to carefully consider our options before we made our decision final. If we went ahead and lost the case, Dad would walk free, completely acquitted of all charges against him. I think the CPS saw the plea bargain as a way of getting a guaranteed positive outcome rather than taking the gamble.

The next day, Jon and I discussed in great depth what to do, but whichever way I looked at it I still preferred to lose the case rather than give in to my father's wishes. I had promised myself that day in York, when my family had let me down once more, that I would never cover for them again, that I would face my past head on – and that was exactly what I was going to do.

Wednesday came and we braced ourselves. Jon and I arrived at the courts, trying our best to maintain a brave front. At ten o'clock we were all called through to the courtroom for the jury to be sworn in. As each member took a seat on the bench I examined every face. These men and women in front of me would decide not just my father's future, but mine as well. My fate was in their hands. I couldn't believe how ordinary members of the public could make such a huge decision about someone's life, and I hoped and prayed that they could see my father for what he really was.

My greatest fear was that my father would be able to manipulate the jury the way he had always manipulated everybody else in his life, the way he had manipulated my brother when confronted with the taped evidence. But as I looked up and saw my father for the first time standing in the dock, I knew that I was equal to him this time. Now, as he hung his head in shame, he appeared a shadow of the man I had built him up to be, barely even looking at his surroundings. Gone was the powerful, successful man I had always seen him as, and in his place was an old man who, to me, looked as guilty as sin. I hoped the jury saw him in the same way.

Once the jury had been sworn in, Jon and I had to wait in the witness room along with all the other witnesses giving evidence that day. This was probably a good thing, as the hum of activity prevented us from having too much time to get worked up prior to giving evidence.

The witness service representative, John Holland, introduced himself. He was amazing to us, always available to answer any questions we had, or just chat with us to pass the time. He was good to us the first time my family passed us in the corridor. It was unrealistic to expect never to bump into them, but the pain I felt when I saw their familiar faces, knowing that my mother and brother were there to support my father and not me, still hurt beyond belief. John Holland kept us busy, not allowing us to dwell on it. My mother and brother didn't even have the courage to enter the courtroom. Throughout the trial they had waited in my father's waiting room for his return, not wanting to hear one word of the truth that was spoken inside that court.

It was John who called me through to give my evidence.

My stomach flipped.

I rose from the chair, grasping Jon's hand as tightly as I could.

We walked through to the courtroom as confidently as we could, united in our objective. Jon took a seat in the public gallery, and an usher showed me to the witness box. I stared straight ahead as I made that short walk, desperate not to make eye contact with anybody, certain that, if I did, I would pass out with complete and utter fear.

I had used the term 'scared' and 'fearful' in the past, but it was only now that I understood what they really meant. Fear runs through you like ice-cold water, practically freezing your veins. I didn't know how to breathe, and I suddenly realised that I had unconsciously been holding my breath for ages. My chest physically hurt, and I tried to regain my composure. I had one chance and I was determined not to blow it.

I was handed the New Testament and a card to read my oath from. With shaking hands I took the Bible in my right hand, reading as firmly as I could: '. . . I swear that the evidence I give shall be the truth, the whole truth and nothing but the truth . . .' The prosecution counsel then rose to his feet. This was a man I had never met before but whom I knew was on my side.

He asked me a series of questions, the answers to which were designed to illustrate to the jury the extent of the abuse that had occurred. I answered every question in a confident voice, as honestly and directly as I could, but inside I was still shaking. I knew I needed to gather every ounce of courage and resolve to make my case clear.

And, suddenly, standing there in that witness box, something happened to me. My panic and apprehension completely left me and was replaced with a confidence and complete ease with the truth. For the first time in this whole horrible business, I realised how easy telling the truth was and that all I had to do was answer the questions about the blunt reality of what had happened. I realised how hard, in comparison, it was going to be for my father. He would have to watch every word he was saying, ensuring that he didn't trip himself up with the lies he would have to tell. I knew I had the upper hand and began to enjoy the opportunity to tell my truth with no denials or interruptions. It was something I wasn't used to.

By the time the defence counsel began his interrogation, I was well and truly on a roll. There wasn't a question put to me that I didn't feel able to answer immediately with confidence and a passion that I hoped proved my integrity. I felt powerful, and willed him to push me further. *Go on, then*, I thought to myself, *try me*. There was nothing the defence counsel could say that I didn't have the answer to. I glanced over towards my father in the dock, hanging his head.

Once my father's QC had completed his questions, the prosecution barrister introduced the tape as his next piece of evidence. A tape recorder was set up and transcripts handed to every member of the jury, me on the stand, the judge and both barristers. As the tape was played, everyone listened intently to the conversation between my father and me. As it came to a close, with the line, 'It's a funny old life, isn't it?' you could have heard a pin drop in that courtroom. Everyone seemed horrified by his callous words. The prosecution barrister turned to me and dismissed me from the stand.

I stepped down, surprised at myself and relieved too that the experience hadn't been nearly as harrowing as I'd expected. As I sat down next to Jon, he turned to me and whispered, 'You were amazing.'

The next day it was Rob's turn to give evidence and he was asked to confirm the details of the case: dates, times, interviews. He was on the stand only a matter of minutes before he was also released from the court. Rob was determined to remain for the entire trial and sat in the public gallery with us. His dedication and support touched us immensely.

Suddenly the barristers began whispering to one another and we were asked to leave the court while they discussed a legal matter. We left in confusion, wondering what on earth was going on. After a few moments an usher appeared, beckoning us back into court. As I walked towards the public gallery, the usher asked me to proceed to the witness stand once more. I was so confused. I'd given my evidence yesterday. Why did they need me again?

I entered the witness stand feeling bewildered and apprehensive. Yesterday's confidence had completely deserted me with this sudden turn of events. The judge apologised for my recall, explaining that the defence had fresh evidence to put to me that had just come to light. I panicked. What on earth did they have? What was going to happen now? Obviously my father's QC had realised he needed to squash my testimony, to taint the confident image I had left the jury with. He looked gleeful as he presented me with a series of photographs of my home in Llechryd, where the abuse had taken place.

'Don't you find it strange, Mrs Latchem-Smith, how there are so many houses close by in that estate, yet you seem convinced that the occurrences happened in the car in broad daylight?'

I could see where this was leading. He was trying to convince the jury that the abuse couldn't have happened because we had been in full view. I knew what he was saying was true. But the truth was all I had.

'Yes, we were most probably in full view, but I can't change the facts just to suit my evidence,' I told him. 'Yes, it would sound more convincing if it had been some dark alleyway somewhere, but that just wasn't the case. I can only tell you the truth, nothing more, nothing less.'

This dialogue continued, with me responding in much the same way over and over again. I could only tell the truth and refused to back down or change my evidence in any way. Eventually, I was once more released from the stand.

Exhausted, I returned to my seat next to Jon and

Yve. 'Well done,' they whispered, and clung on to me in support.

After a break for lunch, the next witness was called forward. My father. As he took the stand, I was determined to face him, to hear him lie through his teeth about me while I watched him and listened to his every word. After the plea-bargaining attempt he had to change his plea to guilty on two charges. He knew the tape would convict him otherwise. I thought how ironic it was that he had offered me four charges under plea bargain, but only two to the jury. I was gutted that I hadn't been able to mention that in court.

When my father took the stand, he was initially asked to confirm his details – name, address and so forth. He was then asked if my account of my mother's behaviour had been fair and correct. He had to admit that my recollections of her behaviour had been accurate, although he put her obsessive tendencies down to a dust allergy. As my father gave his evidence, he constantly pulled at his ear in a nervous twitch. I was amazed by his lack of composure. I had been so sure that he would manipulate the jury and be his usual confident self. The usually self-assured man seemed to have disappeared and in his place was the real Michael. The guilty Michael. A man trying to lie his way out of prison, who appeared to be fighting a losing battle.

Many times he answered a question put to him with, 'I honestly don't know how to answer that,' which reminded me of his dialogue on the tape.

When questioned about the incidents he was admitting to, he claimed that he had only ever touched me twice and that I had taken his hand, placing it between my legs. He claimed that the only thing he was guilty of was leaving it there longer than he should have done and giving way to my advances. I gasped at his words, unable to believe that they had escaped his lips. My surprise didn't go unnoticed. Jon and I were asked to move to the other end of the public gallery, out of the jury's view.

The next day, the two barristers gave their closing speeches to the jury. The prosecution barrister was an older man, softly spoken, and I can't deny that I was disappointed by his quiet summary of my case. My father's QC, in comparison, was impressive. Enthusiasm oozed from every pore as he put forward a fabulous case in my father's favour. He went into minute detail, drawing the jury's attention to my unreliability as a witness because of my previous retractions. Even the jury seemed impressed with his summing up. My heart fell. The defence QC's was the last speech the jury heard and surely it would be his words ringing in their heads whilst they deliberated.

It was Friday and, thankfully, the judge adjourned for the day, asking the jury to return on Monday for his closing words before they reached their verdict. As we went home that night, we dreaded the weekend ahead. The next two days would be the longest we had experienced. There was no more evidence. The jury had heard everything from both sides and all angles. I wondered what was going through their heads as they spent that weekend with their families. They held the power either to put a man in prison, or to leave my life tainted with doubt. I began to dread Monday morning and the reading of the jury's decision.

17

The Final Word

I awoke on Monday morning feeling physically sick. This was potentially the last day of the trial, depending on how long the jury took to consider their verdict. Jon and I made our way to court. On arrival, the courts were busy dealing with incidents from the weekend, and our case was delayed until late morning. I was almost grateful to be kept waiting. The quicker we entered that courtroom, the quicker my whole life might fall apart.

Eventually John Holland let us know that the judge was ready to give his last words to the jury. We walked into the courtroom and sat once more in the public gallery, holding hands tightly, united in our resolve. The judge then spoke to the jury and directed them to the particular facts of my case before releasing them from the court. I watched each one of those jury members leave the room. Inside I was screaming, 'I'm telling the truth! Please believe me!' On the outside, I did my best to paste a weary smile on my face as they took a final glance at me before leaving the room.

Jon and I returned to the witness room for what could be an extremely long wait. The jury had a lot to consider and it was more than likely that we would have to return the next day for their verdict. We went for a short walk into town for some lunch, although I felt too nervous to eat. Instead we wandered up and down the road, desperately trying to waste some time. We returned to the courtroom, knowing full well that the ushers would only return from lunch at two o'clock, so that was the earliest the jury could deliver their decision. This felt like an unrealistic presumption, however, as we knew the wait ahead of us could be far beyond that, but I didn't want to be away from the courtroom, just in case.

Much to our shock, at two o'clock John Holland came rushing in.

'You're not going to believe this – they've got a verdict,' he told us.

Jon and I were rushed through to the courtroom, where we sat right in front of the jury. My heart was beating so fast and so loud I thought everyone would be able to hear it. I couldn't breathe, and I had to try desperately to quieten the noise rising up from my chest for fear of missing the verdicts. The judge asked the jury foreperson to stand. A lady got to her feet.

'Have you reached a verdict on which you are all agreed?' he asked.

'Yes, your honour,' she replied.

Oh, my God, this was really it. A unanimous verdict. I wasn't sure if it was a good sign or a bad one that the decision had been made so quickly. I held on to Jon so tightly my fingers turned white. This was the culmination of everything we had worked towards in our eight years together and I was so scared of it all falling apart now. I braced myself, holding my breath in anticipation.

The court official began his questions . . .

'The defendant already pleads guilty to counts one and two of the indictment, charges of indecent sexual assault. Therefore on count three, indecent sexual assault against a child, how do you find the defendant? Guilty or not guilty?'

'Guilty.'

I fell on to Jon's chest, completely losing control. I began sobbing hysterically as I realised what I was hearing.

'On count four, indecent sexual assault against a child, how do you find the defendant? Guilty or not guilty?'

'Guilty.'

'On count five, indecent sexual assault against a child, how do you find the defendant? Guilty or not guilty?'

'Guilty.'

I didn't know how to react. Emotions crashed over me. My composure fell apart. I continued sobbing in Jon's arms, and he held me tight.

'On count six, gross indecency towards a child, how do you find the defendant? Guilty or not guilty?'

'Guilty.'

'On count seven, gross indecency towards a child, how do you find the defendant? Guilty or not guilty?'

'Guilty.'

'On count eight, gross indecency towards a child, how do you find the defendant? Guilty or not guilty?'

'Guilty.'

'On count nine, gross indecency towards a child, how do you find the defendant? Guilty or not guilty?'

'Guilty.'

'On count ten, attempted rape, how do you find the defendant? Guilty or not guilty?'

This was it, the biggest charge of all. I knew my father was dreading it, as Rob had said that this would be the one above all he would hope to avoid. It guaranteed a gaol sentence.

I somehow managed to lift my head from Jon's chest,

tears still streaming down my cheeks, and I turned to face my father. I had to watch him, see his reaction, see him face the juror's words. If he got away with it, I wanted him to see me and *know* his guilt even if the law didn't recognise it. I was no longer afraid of him. I hated him for what he'd put me through.

'Guilty.'

My father dropped his head, and I broke down completely. Guilty of all ten counts against him. I was sobbing hysterically again, clutching at Jon's shirt as I tried to stop myself collapsing on the floor. I had prepared myself for not guilty verdicts; I could have taken that. But I hadn't been prepared for the massive impact of this moment.

No one could ever again say to me that my father was innocent. Twelve members of a jury had just given me something invaluable – my life back.

We were shown into a private room to regain our composure. My father, instead of walking back to my mum and brother as he had done throughout the trial, instead of returning to the hotel with them that night, was taken down to the cells. People kept coming into our room to congratulate us. I could barely register their faces, let alone their voices. But once we had composed ourselves, we stepped outside of that room into peace. We had won, not just for ourselves, but for anyone else out there who was suffering. We had shown what could be achieved with some grit and determination.

As we passed my father's room, where my mother and brother were seated, I glanced through the glass to see their reaction. My mother was sobbing. My brother had hung his head in despair. I felt nothing.

As we left the courtroom, we passed the jury members leaving the building. I looked each one in the eye and mouthed, 'Thank you,' as I walked past. They stood and watched as Jon and I walked away, their sympathetic smiles and looks following us to our car. We began making calls to our friends and family, to share in our joy. We pulled out of the car park, and made our way to Emlyn to collect our little girls and take them home in the knowledge that they would now be safe from my father for ever.

The sentencing had been adjourned until 25 August. In the period between the trial and the sentencing, I received two letters from my father. In his first, he continued to deny the charges against him, claiming that they were not true, and he could never admit that they were. In the second, however, he seemed more reflective.

Sunday 21 August 2005

Dear Julia,

You are probably not expecting me to write to you again so soon and, if this letter is unwelcome, I will understand if you throw it away unread.

In prison, one has nothing but time. Time to think and to reflect, and to consider the consequences of one's actions. I have hurt the people I love and the hurt has gone on for too long. I do not ask for your forgiveness. God will forgive me if he truly believes in my sorrow. I have spent some time with the prison chaplain and studying the Bible. It is helping me to look inside myself and question my beliefs and feelings.

Julia, I alone cannot make you happy. In all truth I have made you and all my family unhappy, but I want you to have a happier future. If I have to suffer to bring you all peace, then suffer I will.

You have a bright and happy future ahead of you, with a family who love you. Please don't let the past and my part in it get in the way of that happier future.

Julia, I am not asking you to do anything for me. My concern is your future and that of Mum, your brothers and your children. Please don't let bitterness and hate stop you from moving on. I am truly sorry for the past but I cannot expect you to accept that, if it goes against your feelings, but please accept this. My punishment and suffering will be worthless if nothing changes for the better as a result. I wish you and all the members of my family to put aside blame and hate in favour of hope and love.

Please do not reply, as I have no privacy and these thoughts are between you, me and God.

May God bless you and keep you, and give you peace and strength.

Dad

A few days after I received this letter, we returned to court for the sentencing. I was determined to attend, to see this journey through to the very end. Walking back into those court buildings was surreal, all the memories and anguish came flooding back as I remembered the way I had felt there the month before. This time was different. We knew my father would get a custodial sentence, we just didn't know how long it was likely to be.

As we walked into the courtroom, we took our familiar seats. My father was led to the dock and, as he looked over at me, he mouthed the words, 'Are you OK?' I nodded in response, and turned to face the judge to await his fate. The barristers put forward different suggestions and raised legal issues. Eventually a sentence of eight years was decided upon.

I walked out of that room finally feeling as though justice had been done. I still loved my father, regardless of who he was, but I didn't have one ounce of regret for putting him where he deserved to be. Given my time all over again, I would have done exactly the same thing.

As I left Swansea Crown Court for the last time, I took one final look at the forbidding building. I would never forget this place. It had brought me tears and despair, joy and hope. It had tested my strength and resolve in a way I had never before experienced, pushing me to my limits both physically and mentally. It had changed me from a vulnerable girl into a strong woman – the woman I am today. I had won. I had achieved more here in a week than I had in the previous twenty-four years. And for once, I was proud to be me.

With the court case over, and the sentencing confirmed, I could really begin to lay my past to rest. The reality of what we had achieved began to sink in. To go from such an intense state of heightened alert – so much to think about, to worry about – to complete calm and almost emptiness in my life was a hard transition. I had everything I wanted, my husband and children around me and no burden left to carry, yet it was difficult to adjust to life without a focus or drive.

Jon and I felt that we had achieved so much over the past few months, we didn't want to stop. So many other people out there were suffering, as I had suffered, and we knew first-hand how hard that was to deal with, and were determined to try to help in any way we could. We decided that if we could find the opportunity to tell our story and get the message out there, then maybe someone somewhere would benefit from our experience.

Child abuse is something that is increasingly at the forefront of people's minds. That it is a frequent occurrence is now common knowledge, thanks to campaigns by the NSPCC and Childline. Despite this, Jon and I still knew that it was an issue that was hushed up; something that people found too hard to talk about. And many people still misunderstand child abuse. There are expectations in society about the way a victim should react, the way he or she should behave, which is often not consistent with reality. We knew only too well how people had doubted us over the years. Many people still expect a paedophile to be a dirty old man living in a socially deprived area. All too often cases are overlooked because the abuser doesn't fit the criteria or the child is seen as sexually promiscuous because of the conditioning he or she has endured. People conclude that these children are fabricating their story. These were misconceptions that we were determined to rectify. We became determined to raise public awareness, and break the taboo that still surrounds abuse.

If, by finding the courage to tell my own story, just one person could benefit, then I would have achieved my goal. I began to think of what would have made a difference to me when I was little, what would have made me realise what was happening to me.

I realised that simply sharing my story was key. Working with a journalist, I did various press features, appeared on *This Morning* and also a special edition of *Trisha*. But I also sent an email to the NSPCC, offering to help them in any way I could, but was still surprised when I received an email from Belinda, the communications manager at their Cardiff office, asking if we could meet to discuss some ideas I might be interested in contributing to.

We arranged a meeting at the next available opportunity and I drove to Cardiff, eager to discuss what she had in mind. The meeting went well, and we discussed media opportunities to get my story heard in conjunction with their May 2006 sexual abuse campaign.

Belinda asked me if I would be prepared to do audio and video recordings to be used on TV and radio. I was more than happy to contribute, assuring her that when they were ready to proceed I would work with them throughout the campaign.

A few weeks later, I received another call from the NSPCC, but this time from their head office in London. They had a big meeting arranged with the chief executive of ITV, and various other producers and programme managers, to discuss ways of working with the issue of child abuse. They asked me if I would be willing to attend, to give an account of what it's like for the victim, and to give my own suggestions on what would break through to the public and make them more aware of the problems around them. I grabbed the opportunity with both hands.

Jon and I met with the media staff at the NSPCC head office, and travelled with them to the ITV headquarters overlooking the Thames.

There were at least a dozen participants at this meeting, and as we sat around the large circular table we all introduced ourselves and detailed our position. I'd had no real preparation for this. I was just Julia, a twenty-five-year-old mum living in Bridgend. As my turn came, I cleared my throat.

'Hello. My name is Julia, and I'm a survivor of

childhood sexual abuse. I'm here today to hopefully give you all some insight into the experiences of being the victim in an abusive situation, and to guide you through the awareness that still needs to occur in order to combat this problem worldwide.'

It was bizarre. People were listening to me. They were genuinely interested in everything I had to say. I went through my story, answering each question put to me with the clarity and blunt honesty that I knew was exactly what was needed.

Various programme, documentary and soap ideas were thrown about, as each member of the meeting contributed what he or she could to the cause. As Jon and I left the building, we felt honoured to have been a part of such an influential moment. We made our way past Big Ben, through Trafalgar Square, and on to Leicester Square to enjoy the remainder of our evening.

As we sat in a quaint little restaurant, with a bottle of red wine, we took a step back to reflect on all that we had achieved. It was incredible how far we had come. Our lives had changed so much in the space of a year. We made the calls we had promised to friends and family to inform them of how the day had progressed, and they expressed their admiration and respect. As we sauntered back through the city to our hotel, I turned to Jon.

'Thank you for the trust and loyalty you have shown me. You are the one person in my life who has never doubted me, and it's down to you that I'm the person I am, standing here today,' I told him.

Jon's smile shone, and his love for me was apparent in every feature on his face.

'You're worth it,' was his response, and we walked hand in hand through the busy streets of London, content with our life together and the direction it was taking.

Back at home, we continued with our mission. It was ingrained in us by now to continue fighting with a passion. I had taken complete stock of my life, and taken responsibility for my actions past and present. I decided once and for all to let go of the pain and hurt I had carried for too long.

I picked up the receiver, and dialled a number that was still all too familiar.

'Hello?' I heard a voice say.

'Mum. It's Julia.'

I didn't call her to make amends, to invite her back into my life and pick up where we had left off. I called her simply to forgive her. Harbouring the hate I felt towards her was causing me pain. If I was determined to help others – and I so desperately was – it had to be accomplished with a clear and rational head. I had to let go of my mother. It didn't matter that she wasn't a major part of my adult life, that we now had no contact whatsoever. Of course there would always be an emotional attachment between us, as mother and daughter. I would always love my mother in some way, but the fact that I held so much anger towards her, and blamed her for not seeing the abuse I had been subjected to, was hurting me – and only me – and keeping her in my life when all I wanted to do now was move on. By making that call, by forgiving her, I could finally put it behind me.

I explained to her on the phone that I forgave her, that I was prepared to let go of my anger towards her for not protecting and supporting me for my own sake. I expected her to be furious, to shout back with comments that she had done nothing that warranted forgiveness. My mother was a woman who by now was so convinced of her beliefs that she and my father were innocent of any accusations against them, that I didn't expect her to accept my forgiveness. Surprisingly, she simply said, 'Thank you.'

As I replaced the receiver I felt incredibly calm and focused. The anger had in fact dispersed as I'd hoped, although I wasn't naïve enough any more to believe that anything would bring her back. I knew my mother had gone for good, and I felt at peace with that decision I had made. She had chosen where her loyalties lay, and I had at last accepted it.

I know that my mother and my brother, Paul are unable to comprehend the way that I have decided to live my life. I have been accused of sensationalising and capitalising on my past. Those who know me for who I am know that I am not a materialistic person. The work I did for the NSPCC was on a purely voluntary basis and there was no financial reward. I have tried to highlight the issue of abuse using first-hand knowledge and insight that mere statistics are unable to provide. The NSPCC campaign was highly successful and something I shall always be proud of contributing to.

Many people may still believe that I am wrong to have spoken out, but it is this expectation that I should politely bury the past that makes me so passionate about revealing it. I was abused. I have survived. And I shall continue to embrace my past in order to make me a stronger person in the future.

And so here I am. Still just twenty-six years old, married to the most amazing man, with two beautiful daughters and a newborn son to make our family complete. I know I may face many more obstacles along life's way, but I feel strong and equipped to deal with anything life may throw at me. I don't view myself as a victim. I don't even view myself as a survivor. I'm just a woman who has coped with life the only way she knows how. Living in truth has opened up doors to me that I never could have imagined existed. I feel proud to be where I am today, with my head held high. I'm just me. No more. No less. Just 'Julia'.

More non-fiction from Headline

BRAVEMOUTH

PAMELA STEPHENSON

What did Billy and Pamela do next?

Billy, the ground-breaking biography of the nation's favourite iconoclast, gave millions of readers a fascinating insight into the personal and professional life of the genius that is Billy Connolly. Now, in the sequel to that bestselling book, the award-winning Pamela Stephenson celebrates life with the Scottish beastie as he hits the big six-0.

Witty, insightful and intimate, Stephenson's frank and funny portrait of an epically eventful year draws the reader into two very different worlds: hers of international sexology and the serious psychology of humorists, his of incontinence pants, being married to a shrink – and the finer points of banjo playing.

'Full of Pamela Stephenson's trademark
wit and incisiveness' *Observer*

'Stephenson's tales of the family's life are recounted with a frankness that makes the book all the more credible not to mention touching' *Glasgow Herald*

NON-FICTION / BIOGRAPHY 0 7553 1284 8

THE BOY WITH NO SHOES

WILLIAM HORWOOD

The Boy With No Shoes is the story of an extraordinary journey from a past too painful to imagine to a future every child deserves.

Based on bestselling novelist William Horwood's own heartbreaking boyhood in south-east England after the Second World War, this is a triumphant story of a boy's struggle with early trauma and his remarkable journey into adulthood. Using all the skills that went into the creation of his modern classics *Duncton Wood*, *Skallagrigg* and *The Willows in Winter*, Horwood has painted an unforgettable picture of childhood suffering, personal survival and the power of faith and courage to turn darkness into light.

'A beautifully written and deeply moving memoir'
Sunday Times

NON-FICTION / MEMOIR 0 7553 1318 6

Now you can buy any of these other bestselling
non-fiction titles from your bookshop
or *direct from the publisher*.

FREE P&P AND UK DELIVERY
(Overseas and Ireland £3.50 per book)

For the Love of My Mother   John Rodgers   £6.99
The harrowing but ultimately uplifting tale of a young
woman who, though consigned to a Magdalene Laundry and
separated from her baby son, resolves never to give up on life
in the hope of being reunited with him once more.

Don't Wake Me at Doyles   Maura Murphy   £7.99
The remarkable memoir of an ordinary Irish woman and her
extraordinary life. From her early days running wild in the
countryside, to her destructive marriage to a hard-working,
hard-drinking womaniser, the birth of her nine children, and
a life-or-death choice that would change her forever.

Life, Interrupted   James McConnel   £6.99
A memoir of obsession, compulsion, loneliness, alcoholism,
music, the quest for identity, the search for love, some very
fine jokes and late-diagnosed Tourette's.

Pete Doherty: My Prodigal Son   Jacqueline Doherty   £6.99
Nothing can break a mother's love for her only son. The
mother of Britain's most notorious drug addict talks for the
first time about what she calls 'the Peter problem' in a deeply
moving account of his very public self-destruction, and her
endless love and hope for him.

To order, simply call 01235 400 414
visit our website: www.headline.co.uk
or email orders@bookpoint.co.uk

Prices and availability subject to change without notice.